WHEREVER YOU ARE IN THE WORLD

YOU ARE AN INVENTOR

by
Liam M. Birkett

Easy to understand

This book was written as a response to many requests made to me over my years associated with inventions, devising trade marks, creating brands and utilising intellectual property from a sales and marketing perspective. The calls came from clients, readers of my articles, listeners to my radio contributions and especially the many attendees at my seminars.

Entertaining and accessible

All these groups told me repeatedly that they wanted a more detailed record of what I had said or written. Time and again, people came to me saying that my approach was entertaining, easy to understand, and my delivery made the subject matter accessible to everyone.

Relevant internationally

The general principles of Intellectual Property (IP) rights are similar internationally. This is because IP law has largely been harmonised, for example in the EU. However, there will always be exceptions to the general rule in some jurisdictions. Because many of my talks and seminars are given in Ireland, the content frequently cites Irish examples. Nevertheless, these examples are relevant to international situations.

Contents

About the author

Chapter 1: Setting the scene

Chapter 2: The basic essentials

Chapter 3: Testing your skill

Chapter 4: Delving deeper

Chapter 5: Subject matter search

Chapter 6: Patent specification/offices

Chapter 7: Filings and costs

Chapter 8: Benefits of patent pending

Chapter 9: Solo or with a partner

Chapter 10: Filing internationally

Chapter 11: Possible infringers

Chapter 12: Alternative Methods

Chapter 13: The benefits of branding

Chapter 14: Answers to your test

Chapter 15: Design rights

Chapter 16: Copyright

Chapter 17: A cautionary tale

Chapter 18: Copyright vs trade mark

Chapter 19: A Quick review

Chapter 20: Bringing inventiveness to the surface

Chapter 21: Putting it into practise

Chapter 22: What you can achieve

Profile

Liam Birkett is changing the way many people and firms do business. No matter the size of the firm or the budget, his refreshing enthusiasm, insight and expertise create business ideas and turns them into reality.

Liam began in office management before moving into sales and marketing. He was involved in the launch of Mace and VG group in Ireland. His experience extends into wholesale, retail, cash and carry, and consultancy on a national and international basis.

He worked for advertising agency O'Kennedy Brindley Advertising (which became Saatchi & Saatchi) before co-founding design and marketing consultancy Bernardini, Birkett & Gardner Ltd. For more than 20 years, his firm was responsible for corporate identities and marketing initiatives for blue-chip companies and SMEs.

His unique skill is to see matters from a design, marketing and sales perspective. Coupled with his comprehensive understanding of intellectual property, Liam can generate a unique way of looking at existing or new business opportunities.

Many people have good ideas, products or services but do not have the ability to commercialise them. In the absence of a worthwhile promotional fund, they cannot obtain essential media exposure. Liam can show them how to do it. Being the creator of brands and an inventor himself, he has 'been there, done that'.

Liam is sought out as a pundit on intellectual property matters and has been repeatedly asked to speak to university classes, business groups and professional bodies, both national and international.

He is a consultant expert to the European Commission Framework Programme and past president of the Society of Designers in Ireland.

Connect with Liam M Birkett

My website: liammbirkett.com

Like me on Facebook: facebook.com/liammbirkett

Connect with me on LinkedIn: linkedin.com/in/liambirkett

My Smashwords author profile: smashwords.com/profile/view/liamBirkett

For a hard copy of this book see http://www.liammbirkett.com/

Chapter 1: Setting The Scene

Wherever you are in the world -you are an inventor

Yes you are!

Creativity knows no bounds. Wherever you are in the world, whatever you do, you are an inventor. You may not realise it you but you are.

If I can be an inventor so can you.

I have no legal or technical qualifications. I have difficulty putting a plug onto a lead!

Be a doer

But I get ideas. Lots of ideas. And, from time to time, when I leave them on my "mental shelf" I change from a thinker to a doer. Achieve the same transformation yourself - change from a thinker into a doer!

Lots more besides

From the very beginning I set about learning how to patent something. It's not that difficult to understand when you spend a little time at it. Along the way I learned a lot more besides. These are the other sorts of things you can bring into play, besides applying for a patent, when you begin being an inventor and applying for a patent.

Commerciality

These are very important angles that can add hugely to the

commercial success of the idea/concept/invention, call it what you will.

Alone/partnership

Bottom line – will it sell? Can I market it myself? Can I sell it to someone else who will market it? Do I form a partnership with a third party to exploit it?

Questions answered

These are the insights and questions I encountered alone the way. All of the questions, I found answers to and exploited, profitably, to the full.

This is for you

All of this is what I want to share with you. Now. If you will allow me?

Unlock your door

Perhaps you will. Perhaps you won't. For the price of this book you can unlock your mental door to success.

Is this too much to ask of you?

Yes, but how?

Most of us have an idea (or ideas) we believe can make us a fortune. But we do nothing about it. This is because we are unsure of what to do or how to go about it.

Here is your how-to guide

This book is your special friend. The one that will explain and explore all you should do to transform your idea into a reality. Never again will you say "I should have." Instead, it will be I did. It worked."

Simple and easy

No legal jargon is used. It's just a simple, step by step, easy to understand and follow, guide. It starts with the essentials and clearly marks out the path to success.

Many examples

Along the way lots of examples and suggestions are given. These will not only assist you but will also inspire you to even more possibilities.

Realise your ambition

You will become a true inventor. For a relatively modest outlay you can take steps to realising a huge return on your initial investment.

Or sit on the fence

It is your decision to take. Will you simply sit on your idea? Perhaps see someone else do what you had in mind and enjoy the profits? Will you say to yourself, I thought of that but never did anything about it?

Bite the bullet.

Read the book and get started. Today.

Risk/reward

You have very little to lose, yet so much to gain.

Wherever you're located

It does not matter what country you are in, the process is pretty much the same. In this book, you will read about

    - assessing your concept

    - looking at the potential it has in your targeted marketplace

    - how much protection you can have if you proceed.

Various forms of protection

Besides looking at the patent process you will become aware of, and familiar with, other protective mechanisms you can employ.

Design registration

You will see how design registration can give you what you are after. Frequently overlooked, this tool has a number of facets to it that provides interesting levels of exclusivity.

Branding

Then there is the issue of branding, a very robust form of defence. Moreover, registered trade marks can be renewed indefinitely.

Stories galore

Throughout the book a very wide range of stories will help you comprehend how some of the most famous inventions and products came into existence.

Huge sellers

Some of these were patented. Others were not. But the latter still became very popular, were huge sellers and made fortunes for their creators.

Study these in great depth. They will illustrate to you how you can have various levels of protection even if securing a robust patent is not feasible.

Repetition

No apology is made if many of the same points are made on a number of occasions throughout the book. These are made to help you remember what you need to know, and check on, as you go through the process.

Easy access

These points help you to dip in and out of the pages from time to time when you want to check out relevant facts and guidelines.

Wherever you are in the world -you are an inventor.

Chapter 2 - The Basic Essentials

So let's get started.

We begin with examining what can be patented and what cannot. We start with the latter because it will highlight the shortcomings that have to be overcome if something is capable of securing a patent.

You cannot patent an idea per se

Here is an example of a very clever idea. Striped paint is a very good concept. There is a tin of it. You dip in your paint brush, take it out and simply, and easily, paint vertical lines of colour. Red, white and blue; green and gold; pink, orange and lilac; whatever it says on the outside of the tin!

Worldwide

Such an invention would have

- Great marketing potential.

- Worldwide appeal.

- With endless possibilities.

Patent specification

The problem is you don't have the formulation to produce such a combination of colours! If you don't have the "recipe" you cannot make the cake. And a

patent specification is just that, a recipe, so that a person reading it can understand how your invention works.

Technical Effect

Your specification must show exactly how the invention produces the innovative technical effect. In the case of striped paint it's a non-starter.

Although not absolutely essential, nonetheless remembering the old adage "a picture tells a thousand words", it is helpful if you could provide a few drawings to accompany your written description, to help readers understand your invention.

A. Basic Essentials

Here are the essentials

1. It has to be new

2. It has not been disclosed to the public

3. It must have an inventive step

New

This means new, anywhere in the world, as far as you know. You might have seen it in one country but not in another and hope to patent it there – this is not possible.

New means new!

No public disclosure

By this is meant an enabling disclosure. Let me explain this more fully by way of two examples. You will be familiar with the YoYo. Well, if you had invented it and demonstrated it in public, viewers could have figured out how it works. So you would have shot yourself in the foot as far as patent potential is concerned, you have made an enabling exposuret to the public.

Inventive step

To possess an inventive step the invention must have something that is non-obvious to someone "skilled in the art". Simply put, this person is someone who has the skill to understand the subject matter of the invention. For instance, a techie might consider something obvious that would not be obvious to the man on the street.

Chapter 3 Testing Your Skill

Your Tests

Before we go further into the detail, here are a few challenges for you. Can you come up with inventive solutions to the tasks posed below? Remember your invention must satisfy the three essentials

1.   New
2.   No public disclosure
3.   Inventive step

Produce:

1. *A toy with educational and artistic possibilities.*
2. *A travelling companion that ensures a neat appearance for trousers/slacks at all time*
3. *A thermometer that a child will readily allow into their mouth for long enough to get an accurate reading.*
4. *A way of keeping a spring-loaded door open without the use of weights, rope, hooks etc.*

What to avoid

These tests are to stretch your imagination. You must avoid the obvious solutions because that would not satisfy the inventive step requirement. Don't suggest something that is already used as this would not be new and you would fail on two counts.

Solutions that were capable of being patented will be revealed later in the book.

Chapter 4: Delving Deeper

Back to the essentials and greater explanation and detail…

New

Now let us dig into NEW. What already exists is referred to as "the known art". But you could take one or more known arts and use them, in combination, in a non-obvious manner! If this produces a new technical effect it can be classified as NEW.

Public Disclosure

We said that there must have been no enabling disclosure to the public. However, suppose you had invented the first mobile phone. You could have shown the handset in public and pointed out that it was wireless. You might even have given a demonstration of it working "Listen to the weather forecast from New York". The critical element is that the public would not know how your invention worked. Only you knew what went on inside the "black box."

Therefore, no enabling public exposure. Got it?

Inventive step

Claiming that something does not already exist does not necessarily make it inventive. This essential is probably the one most people have the greatest difficulty in understanding.

Clarification

So we should spend a little more time teasing out what's inventive and what's not inventive.

What's not inventive?

As was said earlier the full wording is usually "non-obvious to those skilled in the art." Here's what that means; you might be amazed at how a confectionery chef can produce a perfect meringue. But many other chefs "skilled in the art" can do the same. If they can do it then there is no inventive step.

Bright spark

Likewise, if an electrician can make lights brighten and dim, it might be beyond your knowhow, but other electricians will have the required skill. It's not obvious to you but it is to them and therefore not inventive.

Chin-up

So, from the perspective of inventing, suppose you thought of producing a chin-piece (similar to what's on a violin) for a mobile phone, so that it could be easily held between head and shoulder. That would be new, novel but not inventive.

That's not to say it would not sell and you could make a profit. However, you could not stop a rival from doing the very same or something similar.

What is inventive?

I have an idea for a watch face that has no numerals or hands. However, when you turn it towards you they do appear on the watch face. To add to the attraction I could try to add some extra features to the watch. Suppose the face displayed a family photo, a pet, a graphic? Only when you turn the face of the watch towards your eyes does the time appear.

New – but!

That's new anywhere in the world as far as I know. And it's inventive even though I don't yet know how to make it perform in this manner.

Truly inventive

Watchmakers (those skilled in the art) don't know how to make it perform like this either. But now I have to be inventive and figure out the mechanicals/electronics to bring it to fruition. If I can, I am being truly inventive.

I can then set about seeking a patent.

Chapter 5: Subject Matter Search

Practical Preliminary Steps

Subject matter search

In order to ascertain if your invention has already been thought of and a patent application filed, it is advisable to undertake a subject matter search.

Sites for search

There are a number of important keyword-searchable, free and publicly-accessible web sites you can use to check on previous filings. These are

> http://www.google.com/patents

> http://www.epo.org/searching/free/espacenet.html

> http://www.freepatentsonline.com/

Here's how to use them

Simply type one or more relevant keywords into the textbox (in my example, type "watch face with no numerals or hands") and press "Search". This will lead to a listing of patents (or patent applications) filed, or zero results. If it's the latter things are looking good.

As a side note, for brevity, I will refer to patents and patent applications collectively as "patent documents" for the rest of this book.

Key-words

Vary the search by inserting a variety of key words that might also be used in the description. Using my example, we could try words such as "varying watch-face", "angle-sensitive timepiece viewer", "user-configurable clock display" etc.

Examine any hits

These may produce some hits. You will then have to open each one. There will be a short description of the patent document. This will help you to determine if your invention is outside the scope of the patent documents your search revealed.

Look at the filing dates

While you are looking at each patent document, look to see when they were filed and for which country protection was sought. You will generally see this on the front page of the original copy of the patent document. Alternatively, you will see this in the brief summary provided by the relevant website about the patent document.

We will go into the relevance of this information in more detail later on Page 30. For the moment, so as not to lose our train of thought, we will continue our journey. (With one slight associated observation noted on the next page.)

No search

Some patent attorneys don't bother with searching. There may be lots of reasons for this, but one of them is that there are so many patents filed around the world which never progress through to completion. The reason for this failure to complete may be manifold, for example, the inventor may have run out of money, got distracted, disillusioned or did not have the commitment needed. Alternatively, because of a lack of novelty or inventive step, the patent office may have simply refused to grant a patent for the invention.

Unchallenged

Consequently, the patent applications lapse, perhaps go unpublished and never become a commercial reality.

Similarly, the majority of inventors never police their inventions and so potential infringers can go unchallenged.

Chapter 6: Patent Specification/Offices

Continuing your journey

When you have figured out exactly how to make your invention work you need to set these details out in a patent specification document. This document typically comprises two sections, namely a detailed description of the invention and a claims section. The claims set out the scope of the legal monopoly you are requesting for the invention.

Claims

By their nature (and in contrast with the afore-mentioned detailed description), claims reflect the essence of an invention rather than its detailed attributes. The preparation of a patent specification is best done using the services of a qualified patent attorney.

Costly

Be warned, this can be an expensive undertaking. Professional fees can be daunting, but many patent attorneys offer a first consultation free of charge. During a consultation, it is advisable to ask the patent attorney for an overview of the various stages and schedule of their charges so you can get a sense of the likely costs you will incur along the way.

Professional expertise

By using a patent attorney, you can get a big bang for your buck. They can use their expertise and experience to broaden your protective cover; draft your claims to avoid potential infringement of existing patents and deal with objections that may be raised by the Patent Examiner. The Patent Examiner is the government official responsible for deciding whether to grant, or refuse you a patent.

Those services

A patent attorney will:

> - draft your patent application

> - advise you on the costs and procedures of the available patenting routes (EPO, PCT, national etc.)

> - file your patent application in relevant patent offices

> - handle all the stages of the patenting process (including arguing with the patent examiner as to the merits of an invention relative to cited prior art) all the way right through to grant

DIY at least in part

If your finances are limited, you can undertake at least some of the patenting steps yourself. For example, many patent offices allow you to file an application without the need for a patent attorney.

DIY limits

Before attempting to go it alone, you should check with the relevant patent offices for which activities they will allow you to do yourself and those for which you need to be represented by a patent attorney.

Going it alone-at least in part

For the purpose of this book we are going to assume, for reason of lack of finance, or otherwise, you are going to do it yourself. We will therefore provide you with a step by step explanation and guide to the patenting process. Along the way we will look at some alternative options to seeking patent protection and the reasons for so doing.

Patent Offices

One of the first things to remember about patent filing is that patents are territorial. In other words, a patent granted for an invention in one country will not prevent someone from making, using or selling the invention in another country. Thus, you should try to match your patent filing strategy to your business strategy, so that you file patents for your invention in those countries where you think you are going to make the most money from your invention.

Charges for each country

While the natural first thought is, "I'll go ahead and file patent applications in every country possible then", it is worth remembering that costs are payable at each country in which the patent application is filed. As will be seen later, these costs will build up quite considerably should you file in several countries. So, be smart with your money and only file a patent application in a country where you think the commercial benefits of the invention at least equates with the cost of the filing.

Patent office guidance

Each country has its own Patent Office. This is where you will file your patent application. Pretty much all Patent Office websites provide information, guidance and forms, to help you go about drafting and filing your application.

Patent office sites

Here are a few of the more popularly used sites.

USA (http://www.uspto.gov/patents/)

UK (https://www.gov.uk/intellectual-property/patents)

Ireland (https://www.patentsoffice.ie/en/)

Australia (http://www.ipaustralia.gov.au/)

Templates supplied

As mentioned above, most of these (and other similar) websites have helpful guides explaining how to draft and file a patent application. In many cases, they even provide samples of specifications of various types of patents that have been filed. These will show you how to word and layout your submission. You can use these as a template for your purposes and to become familiar with the expressions used to describe the functionality of each invention.

Instructions provided

Most of these sites are very user friendly and address all of the questions you are likely to raise. The sites will also provide easy-to-understand instructions explaining how to file your patent application and the official filing fee that must be paid together with the patent application.

Chapter 7: Filings And Costs

Priority date

We mentioned earlier the importance of matching your patent filing strategy with your business strategy, particularly in relation to determining the countries in which to file patent applications for your invention. However, what if you haven't really worked out your business strategy yet (i.e. you don't yet know where you're going to make and/or sell your invention)? Don't worry, you don't have to decide at the very outset all of the countries in which to file your patent applications.

File in only one country

The Paris Convention is an international agreement whereby each signatory country (most of the countries in the world) has agreed to recognize the filing date of an application filed in another signatory country.

12 months to decide

This allows you to file a first application for your invention in one country and then, within a period of 12 months from that filing, file subsequent applications for the same invention in other countries so that these subsequent filings can benefit from the filing date of the first filing.

First filing

Don't be put off if this sounds very complicated. We will work our way through this in the following sections. The main thing to think about right now, is filing an application for your invention in a single first patent office. For simplicity, we will call this filing your "first filing".

Pole position

The patent office in which you make your first filing will supply you with the date on which your application, official forms and fee etc. was received by the patent office. This date is known technically as a "Priority Date".

Priority date

This Priority Date is HUGELY important to you. By making your first filing you effectively stake your claim to the territory of your invention. Once you have secured your priority date, no one else can legally patent your invention in virtually any other country worldwide. If someone else later files an application for the same invention as yours, their application will be refused because of your earlier priority date.

You could now skip to page 58 to read a DIY route

Chapter 8: Benefits Of Patent Pending

Patent pending

Once you receive your official filing date you can enjoy the "Patent pending" status. This you can use to your advantage when disclosing/discussing your invention with others (which you can do now with impunity); in correspondence, print material, presentations to third parties; or wherever.

Strong deterrent

The "Patent Pending" designation is a strong deterrent to others who might be tempted to copy or infringe what it is you have or intend to produce.

12 months to "suck it and see"

You are now faced with a number of attractive options to consider. The first of these, as we set out above, is that you can publicly disclose your invention. Because of your first filing, they cannot legally steal your idea or try to patent it themselves.

Acceptance and price point

You can also assess your invention's commerciality. You can do some market research to establish its acceptability and possible selling price.

Not yet granted

Before going any further, it is important to clear up a common misconception – filing a patent application is NOT the same thing as having a patent granted. Unfortunately, the patenting process is considerably more protracted involving many twists and turns. But for right now, under the Paris Convention agreement, you have the best part of 12 months to decide how you intend to proceed.

Match patent to business strategy

Let's go back to the idea of matching your patent strategy to your business strategy. If you feel that your invention will only sell in one country, then, before the 12 months expire, you should do whatever is needed to complete the patent application filing process in that country.

Allow several months

The website for the relevant patent office will generally provide whatever information you need to help you with this. It is advisable to give yourself several months ahead of the final deadline. This will allow for administrative matters that can arise.

Multi-country filings

In the event you are confident that your invention has strong potential in a number of countries, then as previously discussed, you must file in each of those countries.

Big call on funding

To benefit from the priority date (from your first filing) you must file your patent application in each of the relevant countries ahead of the above-mentioned 12 month deadline. But in so doing, you will encounter a big call on funding.

Costly

Filing a patent application in each country will cost you many thousands of dollars, pounds, euro or whatever currency applies.

This is something you should plan from the beginning, because you will have already made some investment.

<u>Again – don't miss the 12 month deadline!</u>

Back dating

As previously discussed, under the Paris Convention Agreement, patent applications filed in whichever countries you choose can claim benefit of the priority date of your first filing. The benefit of this facility is that it's as if you filed in all these countries from the very beginning. Whereas in reality you made your first filing in only country; and you had almost 12 months to "suck it and see". This allowed you time for research and deliberations before incurring the extra expense of multi country filings.

Securing your potential

This is a terrific benefit. For the relatively modest investment of filing in your original country, you have secured your potential in all the additional countries.

Let's look at the costs

If you draft and file yourself then you have only to pay the official filing fees.

Here is a selection of PO filing costs (correct as of the date of writing):

<u>UK</u>: £20 (filing online), £30 (filing by post)

<u>USA</u>: $280, $140 (for small entity filers), $70 (for micro-entity filers)

Ireland: Short Term Patent (60 €), Full Term Patent (125 €)

After that....

However, further fees are incurred at specific time intervals as the patent applications progress to grant. These fees include, for example, excess claims fees, search fee, examination fee, grant/allowance fee etc. The specific fees, their cost and payment deadlines vary from one country to another. To give you an idea of the scale of the costs, the search fee and examination fee for a UK patent application is £130 and £80 respectively if submitted online.

Advance warning

The relevant patent offices will generally send you communications giving you advance warning of the fees payable for a patent application and relevant deadlines for paying the fees.

Ongoing costs

A patent has a lifetime of 20 years from the filing date of the patent application. During this period, further fees are payable at regular intervals to keep the patent alive. The renewal fees ramp up with the number of years since filing.

UK renewal fees

The renewal fees for a UK patent at the 4th, 10th and 15th anniversaries of the filing date are £70, £170 and £350 respectively.

Australian renewal fees

Similarly, for an Australian patent, the renewal fees payable at the

4th, 10th and 15th anniversaries of the filing date are AU\$300, AU\$500 and AU\$1,120 respectively.

US renewal fees

For a US patent, renewal fees are payable three times during the lifetime of the patent, namely at 3 to 3.5 years after the date of issue, 7 to 7.5 years after the date of issue; and 11 to 11.5 years after the date of issue. For a small entity, the renewal fees are currently \$800, \$1,800 and \$3,700 respectively.

Planning your budget

Fees can rapidly build up, particularly if you have filed patent applications in several countries. So even though it might seem like an awfully long time-scale, planning your patent budget (and determining how you are going to fund the expansion of your patent application into multiple countries) is absolutely essential.

Funding the venture

It may well be that you have sufficient funds yourself to handle this expenditure. If so, great, you will own the invention in its entirety at this stage. However, if you do not have the resources to fund the venture, you may need to join forces with someone else (see Chapter 9) or look for other sources of finance.

Additional demands

As time progresses, you will need more money. As well as fees incurred for the patent, there may also be tooling costs, production runs, print and packaging; and advertising - the list can be long and demanding.

Financial assistance

There are a number of options for you to consider. In some countries, State funding is available to assist entrepreneurs to bring such projects to fruition.

Seek them out

Investigate these options because they can be a great source of assistance in a myriad of ways.

List of state agencies

> 1. Innovate UK (formerly the Technology Strategy Board) (www.gov.uk/government/organisations/innovate-uk)
>
> 2. Scottish Enterprise (www.scottish-enterprise.com)
>
> 3. Enterprise Northern Ireland (www.enterpriseni.com)
>
> 4. Australia Business Financing Centre (www.australiangovernmentgrants.org)
>
> 5. United States Patent and Trademark Office (www.uspto.gov/inventors/independent)
>
> 6. Enterprise Ireland (www.enterprise-ireland.com)

Chapter 9: Solo Or With A Partner

Find a partner

You could join forces with someone else to help with the financial investment. This could be a friend or acquaintance that has the funds and would be willing to back your venture.

Equity split

The investor may be prepared to just lend you the money if you are friends. However, usually an investment is made in return for a share in the equity of the venture. This will have to be agreed through negotiation. It could be 5%, 10%, 50% or more - whatever both sides are content with to get the show on the road.

Realise your dream

The expression "half a cake is better than no cake" comes to mind. If you have to part with some of the action to see your dream realised, it is better than to have it die.

Additional expertise

A good piece of advice is to try to find someone who can bring more than just money to the table. It is much better if your partner has an expertise in manufacturing, marketing or finance and/or has valuable commercial connections to help your project come to fruition.

Venture capitalists

There are venture capitalists (VCs) who specialise in taking equity stakes in enterprises such as yours. There are many books devoted to this subject. It would serve you well to delve into a few of them. There is much to learn about the pros and cons of getting finance.

Sell your invention

Another strategy is to try to sell out entirely at an early stage. That way you reap a reward and avoid all of the trials, tribulations and costs of further involvement. There can be a number of strands to this decision.

Structures

You could go for an outright sale. Or perhaps opt for an up-front payment plus royalties on sales. In this scenario it is vital that the terms are clearly set out in a legal agreement. For example, the agreement can stipulate that you get paid a minimum amount every month, quarter, six months or yearly. That way the third party cannot simply sit on the project after the down-payment and you receive no further income.

Motives

Be careful of why someone wants to invest in your venture. A potential "partner" may want to suppress your invention in favour of whatever he/she is already marketing. They may also run into financial trouble or just get lazy. It happens! Securing the interest a third party usually involves a number of considerations.

Level of interest

At the outset your invention has to grab their attention. Then they are likely to want to see the patent. If you have drafted the patent application yourself it is not going to be as impressive as if it was completed by a patent attorney. However, that in itself may not be a deterrent to forging a deal.

Know-how

Your potential partner may be experienced enough to read and understand your patent application and the scope of its protection. If not, he/she can enlist the help of someone who is so skilled. Either way you are still covered by the patent pending designation.

To continue

Now, to return to the patent process. Do not let the 12 month deadline pass before deciding how to proceed.

Here's how to move matters forward. Your decision may be to

> 1. File in one country
>
> 2. File in multiple countries

Either way the filings will be back dated to the date of the filing in the first country.

Claim the benefit

Don't miss the 12 month deadline because otherwise, any applications you subsequently file for the same invention will no longer be able to claim the benefit of the priority date.

Undecided

It is conceivable that as you approach the 12 month deadline, you're still not sure about the countries in which you intend to sell the invention (or even the sources of finance to cover the cost of filing the patent application in the relevant countries).

There are options

Don't worry; you're not the first person to find yourself in this position. There are options that can help, i.e. the European Patent Convention and the Patent Co-operation Treaty, which are discussed in the next chapter.

Chapter 10: Filing Internationally

One filing many countries

The premise behind the European Patent Convention and the Patent Co-operation Treaty is the notion that rather than filing a patent application at individual patent offices before the 12 month deadline, you can file at a single patent office, whose authority covers a number of different countries. This is a cost-effective option when you are seeking protection in more than 3 countries.

Benefits

This has a number of benefits, a few of which are outlined below:

- most of the handling of the patent application is done by one body, rather than a number of independent national patent offices acting, in many cases, substantially in parallel

- it may avoid the necessity of working in multiple languages with the national patent offices

- it may have significant cost benefits compared with filing in individual patent offices (particularly if you are going to file in a large number of countries)

- in effect it allows you to further delay decisions on the countries in which to get your patent granted.

European Patent Convention (EPC)

The EPC allows a single patent application filed at the European Patent Office (EPO), in Munich or The Hague, to be used to obtain a European Patent, covering up to 40 countries (at time of writing), namely

• Albania	• Lithuania
• Austria	• Luxembourg
• Belgium	• Macedonia
• Bosnia and Hercegovina	• Malta
• Bulgaria	• Monaco
• Croatia	• Montenegro
• Cyprus	• The Netherlands
• Czech Republic	• Norway
• Denmark	• Poland
• Estonia	• Portugal
• Finland	• Romania
• France	• San Marino
• Germany	• Serbia
• Greece	• Slovakia
• Hungary	• Slovenia
• Iceland	• Spain
• Ireland	• Sweden
• Italy	• Switzerland
• Latvia	• Turkey
• Liechtenstein	• United Kingdom

Single European patent

European patent applications can be filed in English, French or German and undergo a rigorous search and examination procedure. If the Application gets through this process, the EPO grants a single European patent for the invention, covering all of the 40 states that have been designated by the Applicant.

Validate in each state

The patent owner must validate the European patent in each state in which they want the patent to be valid. If you don't validate the Patent in a particular state before the required deadline, then the protection in that state lapses.

Bundle of rights

The European patent is effectively a bundle of national patent rights. Each of the national rights is dealt with under that relevant nation's laws (and language requirements).

National courts

If there is any subsequent litigation (namely infringement and revocation actions) it must be conducted separately in the national courts for each of the relevant states. Similarly, the national rights exist as separate entities kept in force by the payment of separate renewal fees to the patent offices of each relevant state.

Most cost-effective

If you are thinking of obtaining patent protection in three or more European countries, European patent applications are generally more cost-effective than filing individual applications in each state.

Options open for longer

A European Patent Application keeps your options open for longer, which gives you more time to decide on which countries you want to secure patent rights.

If problems arise

However, the European Patent Convention requires that a person whose residence or place of business is not within the territory of one of the EPC contracting states must be represented by a professional representative for all proceedings that arise <u>after</u> the filing of a European patent application.

Unitary Patent

As an aside, you may have heard some discussions about a so-called "Unitary European Patent". This is another form of European Patent also granted by the EPO. When granted it will stay as a single right covering all EU member states which have ratified the Unified Patent Court ("UPC") Agreement. The unitary patent will not be available until all of 13 member states including the UK, France and Germany have ratified the UPC agreement.

<u>Patent Cooperation Treaty (PCT)</u>

The European Patent Convention is fine for European countries. But what if you're thinking about securing patent rights in the United States or in Asia, but can't decide on it before the 12 month deadline from the priority date?

There is a way to extend that 12 month deadline – but at an additional cost! The PCT is an international treaty with more than 145 Contracting States (including the United States, Asia and Australia). The PCT makes it possible to simultaneously seek patent protection for an invention in a large number of countries.

One language

You can file a single 'international' (or PCT) patent application (at most patent offices) in English, instead of filing separate national patent applications in each relevant national language. In the national phase (discussed later) it may be necessary to file in the language of the country in which the application is being filed.

Different phases

The PCT application is processed through two basic stages, the *international phase* and the *national* (for example, seeking a UK patent) or *regional* (for example, seeking a regional European patent) *phase*.

International phase

During the international phase, your PCT application is searched and published. This takes the place of the many individual foreign patent applications that would otherwise be required for protection abroad. In other words, the PCT application has the same effect as making national patent applications in the individual national patent offices of the PCT contracting states you select.

Different periods, different countries

During the international phase, you have 30-31 months for most contracting states (in Australia, it lasts up to 31 months; in the UK, the US and Japan, it lasts 30 months) before you have to specify the individual countries in which you will seek a patent.

National/regional phase

After that period, the PCT application enters the national or regional phase. During this time, the PCT application is converted into individual foreign patent applications, one in each country or region where patent protection is sought. These patent applications may then be pursued individually to obtain foreign patents.

Extended Deadline

Therefore the PCT system adds another 18 months (on top of the 12) before having to nominate the countries in which you will file.

No international patent

You should note that there is no such thing as an 'international patent'. Patents granted under the PCT scheme remain under the control of the national or regional patent offices in the national/regional phase.

Worth considering

The cost of this is approximately an extra 3,500 Euro. It may be something for you and/or your investor to consider exercising when you are evaluating the potential for sales in various countries.

What happens when a patent application is filed?

While patent offices vary on the details and timing of their procedures, they largely follow similar processes. For example, when a patent application is filed, patent examiners will check all relevant pages have been submitted and that drawings are of a sufficient quality.

Claims search

When the formalities have been checked, the patent examiners conduct a search of the claims in the application to determine whether any identical or very similar invention to the claimed invention has been described in other documents published before the filing date of the patent application.

Prior art

These earlier documents are known as 'prior art'. The patent office issues a search report to the applicant that lists any prior art documents found and an indication of how relevant the prior art is to the claimed invention.

Publication

Approximately 18 months after the priority date, the patent office also publishes the application, which can then be read by members of the public. Prior to publication, the patent application remains confidential.

You can choose to withdraw the application so the details are not published. We will talk further about such options later (see Chapter 12).

Public disclosure

If you want patent protection for your invention, it is a legal requirement that your application discloses how the invention works. Albeit, that the invention won't be disclosed to the public until publication at 18 months from the priority date.

Trade secret

Instead, depending on the nature of the invention, you may decide to protect the invention by way of a trade secret. This is primarily governed by contract law, and is outside the scope of this book.

Substantive examination

After the patent office has searched the application, it will conduct a substantive examination. The patent examiner will give a detailed assessment of the patentability of the invention in light of any prior art.

Arguments

In some instances, the patent examiner will argue that the claimed invention lacks novelty or inventiveness because of the prior art. The applicant is given an opportunity to respond either by arguing that the examiner is mistaken and/or by amending the patent claims to overcome the objection.

To and fro

The patent examiner may respond to the applicant by accepting their arguments and/or amendments. Alternatively, the examiner may reject the applicant's arguments and/or amendments (and may even raise new objections).

Grants or refuses

The cycle of the examiner's opinion and the applicant's response may continue for a number of iterations, until the examiner accepts the resulting application (and grants the patent) or refuses to grant the patent. Meanwhile you continue to enjoy "Patent Pending" status.

Lifetime of a patent

Regardless of the route taken to get a patent granted (national filing, European Patent Office or PCT) the lifetime of a patent is usually 20 years. There are some exceptions to this rule.

Utility Models

Some countries (including Germany, Australia and Japan) also provide patent protection through 'utility models'. These are very similar to a patent but typically have a much shorter duration (about 10 years, although it varies from one country to another) and less stringent requirements.

Short-term patent

The Irish equivalent of a utility model is the 'short-term' patent. It has a lifetime of 10 years and the level of inventiveness required is less than that required for the regular 20-year patent.

Ireland only

If you think your invention may not fully meet the criteria for a 20 year patent, this may be the way to go. Remember, it only applies to Ireland.

Human/veterinary/plant

Another exception to the 20-year period relates to human or veterinary medicines and plant protection products (for example, herbicides). Supplementary Protection Certificates (SPCs) come into force after the expiry of a patent for these inventions. They effectively extend the duration of the patent, up to a maximum of five years in most cases.

Clinical trials

SPCs were devised to compensate for the long time needed to obtain regulatory approval (for example, through clinical trials) for these products.

Protected countries

Wherever you are granted a patent (and this can take many years in some countries) those countries are ring-fenced for the lifetime of the patent.

Ring-fenced

During that period no one can legally manufacture or market your invention in that protected area.

Chapter 11: Possible Infringers

Infringer

If a potential rival appears to infringe your invention in a country where you have been granted patent protection, there are certain procedures to follow.

Cease and desist

You need to write a 'cease and desist' letter to the alleged offender advising them of your patent situation. It is also possible to put a potential infringer on notice that you have filed for a patent, even if it has not been granted yet. However, the wording of these letters needs great care. Patent laws can vary from one country to another. It is best to seek legal advice in this matter.

Take action

If the alleged offender ignores your cease and desist letter and continues to make/use/sell your invention, it is open to you to sue the offender for patent infringement. Again, be guided by your legal advisor to determine the best course of action.

Penalties

Should you successfully bring an action for infringement, the consequences can be severe. Once the offender has been put on notice (by way of the cease and desist letter) the clock starts ticking. Punishment can take many forms. These include:

> - obtaining an injunction to prevent the offender from continuing with the infringement

- seeking damages in respect of the infringement or the profits they accrued from their infringing activity

- delivery up or destruction of the infringing product

Only when patent is granted

However, you can only bring an action for patent infringement against an offender when a patent has been granted for the relevant invention.

Territorial

Since patents are territorial, a patent infringement action in one country will not stop the offender from making, using or selling your invention in another country. So it may be necessary to bring actions in multiple countries.

Chapter 12: Alternative Methods

Alternative routes to market

There are ways to exploit your invention that do not involve actually securing a patent. You may choose to do this because you don't want to incur the financial outlay, run the risk, share equity or cede control of your destiny. You may also consider you have little chance of obtaining a patent.

Evasive action

Start by drafting a patent specification yourself. Most patent office websites have guidelines and examples for you to follow as to how to draft a patent specification. You then file it, without necessarily having the intention of completing the process or even if you lack the confidence that the patent would be granted.

Reducing the down-side risk

You could, for instance, file in the UK. You would do this because there is no cost incurred at the time of filing. The UK Patent Office only seeks a fee towards the end of the first 12 months from filing.

To and fro

It can take many months for a patent office to respond to your submission. In its examination reports, the patent office may raise objections against your patent application, which you can reply to and rebut their arguments. This correspondence can bounce back and forward for a very long time, during which time you have patent pending status.

18 months

You can exploit your patent pending status in your marketing efforts. Your application is held in secret by the patent office for 18 months. As a consequence members of the public (and potential rivals) cannot get to see the details of your invention.

First to market

This gives what sometimes proves to be the marketing edge over rivals at the critical start-up phase. It can provide the 'first to market' advantage that is invaluable.

Blowing smoke

You are in effect putting up a smoke screen. It provides you with a form of protection under which to work.

Scaring rivals

Almost everyone is scared of infringing a patent. People can get sued for millions, which is enough to scare off the most courageous of possible transgressors.

Withdraw your application

The smoke screen cannot be lifted for 18 months. In fact, it may be that your specification is never disclosed to the public <u>because you withdraw your application ahead of publication.</u>

Chapter 13: The Benefits Of Branding

Be first and brand it

I am a great disciple of trade mark registration. Part of my philosophy is that consumers don't buy patents or registered designs (which will be covered on Page 95) -they buy brands.

Inspiring confidence

How often have you heard someone say "I bought it because it's patented"? As opposed to them saying, "I always buy, Nike, Coca Cola, Rolex, Toyota, Kelloggs."

There is an obsession to seek out a trade mark that you can be confident about, one that provides a level of reliability and assurance of quality.

You too

You can capitalise on this too. If you bring something to the market, that offers the consumer benefits, – and brand it – you will build a following.

Trust

Your loyal purchasers won't ask if it's protected by a patent, they will stay with the brand they trust to deliver the benefits they are seeking.

Brand power

Here is a classic example.

We can go into business together and produce a ring-binder containing lined pages. We might sell some of them – but not for $100 or €100 each. Why? Because it's not a *Filofax*! Yet, essentially, a *Filofax* is a ring binder containing lined pages.

Quality and stature

The difference is the branding. The trade marked name and the reputation for quality that accompanies it, raises it to premium price level. It bestows an indication of stature on whoever uses them.

The same can be yours

This highlights the added value that well-chosen, registered, branding can give to your offering.

Expand on this theme

To drive these points home, I want to expand on this theme. To do so, I'm including extracts from my other book entitled

"How to create your trade mark, protect it, and build your brand"

To your great advantage

These extracts go into the matter at some length and discuss many of the attributes that greatly benefit your invention. All this works whether you go down the patenting route or not.

CAN YOU USE AND PROTECT YOUR PROPOSED BRANDING?

On the following pages we go through all of the steps that are required to secure the exclusivity you want.

Trade mark use

A trade mark provides exclusive statutory rights so that a rival cannot legally use an identical or *confusingly similar* trade mark to an earlier registration. On the other hand, if you infringe, then all the investment in design, printing and promotion may be wasted.

Golden Rule

Therefore, the golden rule is, do not attempt to market goods or services until the identity under which you intend to trade has been cleared for use. That is, that it does not conflict with an earlier trade

Search of Trade Mark Registers

It is essential that, before using a new identity, a search is made of the target markets (be that Ireland, the UK, the EU or further afield) to ensure that it does not infringe the rights of others. Expert advice, such as that of a Trade Mark Attorney, is advisable because what appears to be clear to the untrained eye may, in fact, conceal a sustainable objection from a rival.

The registration process

Trade marks are generally registered on a country-by-country basis. However, the Community Trade Mark enables the user by means of a single filing to register its trade mark across the entire territory of the EU.

Four stages

While the application process varies from country to country, most countries provide for four basic stages in its trade mark registration process. These are: Filing by the applicant or his agent, examination by the Patents Office, publication in the Trade

Marks Journal (when third parties can submit objections to the registration of the mark) and registration (by the Patent Office).

Filing

Firstly, the user must fill out a trade mark application form. Most countries now provide for online filing, including online payment of application fees. The application will need to include the basic relevant information such as the identification of the trade mark (e.g. word mark, a specimen of any logo, etc.), the name and details of the applicant (including if the applicant is a person or company entity), a list of the goods or services for which protection is sought, and payment of the relevant application fees.

Nomination of classes

Trade marks are protected by reference to the classes of goods and/or services in which they will be traded. And so the actual list of these classes must be included by the applicant. Most trademark offices provide information online that identify these classes.

45 separate classes

The system is governed by the Nice Classification which divides goods and services into 45 separate classes comprising thirty-four classes of goods and eleven classes of services. The applicant must nominate his chosen classes (e.g. Class 25 covers footwear and clothing while electronic goods such as computers are in class 9.)

Be specific as to intended use

Following a recent EU court decision, registries will no longer automatically allow a user to simply select the standard terms set out in the Nice Classification system. That is the lengthy list of goods and services listed under each class member. As a result, a user may need to liaise with the registry (or consult a professional) in order to put together an acceptable list of goods or services. The general approach is to include those goods/services for which the trade mark is being used or which it is intended to use the mark.

Examination

After a trade mark application has been file it will be examined by an examiner at the relevant trade mark registry. The extent of examination varies widely from country to country. All registries will check to ensure that basic requirements are met e.g. that the mark is not generic, or offends against public morals, or that the list of goods and services is clear and meets its requirements.

In Ireland

Some registries will also conduct a search for earlier conflicting marks. In some cases, such as Ireland, if a search reveals an earlier conflicting mark, the examiner will object to registration. In such instances, the examiner will write to the applicant to explain the reasons for the objection, giving the applicant an opportunity to respond.

UK, EU and elsewhere

In other countries, such as the UK, the Patent Office will not object to registration if its search uncovers an earlier conflicting mark. It will provide the results of its search to the user and the Examiner will also notify the owners of earlier marks who may then choose to object to the application.

Publication – opportunity for objection

After an application has been examined and any issues or problems have been dealt with, most countries' registries will publish the application in an official bulletin (or online) for a period of time (usually 3 months) in order to give others an opportunity to object to registration. A registration gives significant exclusive rights to the owner and so it is considered important to ensure that a procedure exists to allow others to object to registration before it matures to registration.

Opposition procedure

In Ireland and before the EU Trade Marks Office, the period – the opposition period – is 3 months. Usually an opposition is lodged by a person who believes that the published mark is too similar to their earlier mark. Some registries, including Ireland, allow for an opposition to be lodged based on a wide variety of grounds. An opposition triggers an opposition procedure which is handled and decided by the registry in which both sides file arguments and which can include an oral hearing. An opposition can delay registration by a few years and, if successful, would mean the refusal of the application by the registry.

Serious matter

This is why a threat of opposition received from a person who has noticed your application upon publication should normally be taken seriously because an opposition, if filed, could seriously threaten the chances of getting a registration and, at the very least, lead to significant delay and costs for the registration process.

Registration

Assuming the mark has been accepted by the registry – following examination – and has not been opposed before the end of the publication period, it will then mature into registration. Most countries do not provide for payment of fees upon registration and, in such instances, the mark will automatically mature to registration within a short period after the end of the opposition period. The registry will enter the mark on the register and will send the official registration certificate to the owner setting out the details of the registration.

Other countries, such as Ireland, will not register the mark until payment of registration fees. Once registered, the mark will be protected for a fixed period of time which in most countries is ten years from the date of filing.

10 year duration, renewable

The mark can be renewed before the end of each subsequent registration period (i.e. usually even ten years). Most patent and trademark offices provide for payment of a fee upon renewal.

Possible cancellation due to non-use

In most countries a registered trademark will not be automatically cancelled if not used, but instead, it becomes vulnerable to cancellation (usually after a period of 5 years) if it is not put to use for the protected goods or services. The use period varies from country to country. Most have either a 3 or 5 year non-use grace period.

Be aware of local requirements

It is vital therefore to ensure that you are aware of, and comply with, the use requirements in the countries in which the mark has been registered. Otherwise, the registration might lapse for failure to comply with registry requirements regarding maintenance of a registered trade mark.

Secure your position

Once it has been established that the way is clear the mark should be applied for registration immediately and so secure the position.

Territorial

Remember too that registration is territorial, that is, the protection exists only in the countries in which you have a registration. A registration in the United Kingdom extends to Northern Ireland but the Republic of Ireland is another jurisdiction and therefore requires a separate registration.

Export markets

As has been pointed out already, trade mark protection is territorial so, while you may have your mark legally registered in one country it does not mean you can export goods or services carrying this mark to another country.

Prior rights

Many marketers come unstuck at this point. There have been cases where goods were exported to another country, went on sale, only to find that the exporter or the local agent received a "cease and desist" letter from an indigenous company or its legal advisors. The local company had established prior rights to the trade mark in question.

Foreign Language

An offence can be that the trade mark is identical to, or looks, sounds or could be confused with, a trade mark on that local register. On the foreign markets, where there are language differences, the conflicting marks may be spelt differently and appear to the eye to be miles apart, but to the ear, confusingly similar. The overall impression given by the marks at issue is similar!

Local expertise needed

The lesson to be learned therefore is to have the search made by someone who is versed in the language of the target mark and thus obviate this regularly occurring problem.

Use of TM and ®

When you begin to use your brand name you may use the TM sign beside it. This simply stands for trade mark albeit that it is unregistered. However, many people believe it does signify registration and may avoid copying it.

In some countries such as Ireland and the UK it is not until you have obtained a registration of your trade mark that you can legally use the ® symbol for the registered goods or services (unless, for example, you can show that such use refers to a foreign registration.)

Generally it should be used in markets where you have been granted registration. The ruling is different in some other countries and local guidance should be sought.

You now know the process to follow to register a trade mark in individual countries.

You know that trade marks are territorial.

However, in the European Union there is one facility that allows you, with just one application, to apply to register your mark across the EU. This refers to the Community Trade Mark (CTM).

PROTECT YOUR MARK IN THE EU

On the following pages are details that refer to this attractive facility.

Community Trade Mark

In the past when registration was being sought in Europe it was necessary to file country by country. Following the creation of what is now known as the European Union moves were made to provide a short cut. In 1994 a new law was passed that gave us a process whereby a trade mark could be registered Europe wide.

28 countries

Utilising the Community Trade Mark (CTM) it is now possible, with only one application, to apply to register a trade mark in all 28 countries of the European Union.

Anyone who currently trades, or intends to trade, in the EU in the foreseeable future should seriously consider this option. This facility has an added benefit in that when one successfully secures a CTM registration, it is generally considered that it is only necessary to use the mark in ONE of the 28 countries to initially maintain exclusive protection in all member states. (This is available for five years before open to challenge on grounds of non-use.)

Huge market

This opens up huge possibilities for the entrepreneur. This marketplace has about 500 million consumers, making it larger than the United States. As new states join the Community the figure will grow even larger.

There are many benefits to be derived from securing a Community Trade Mark.

Here we itemise and examine them. They will illustrate how you can capitalise on this facility if you have the intention to export your product or service.

Not only do you secure your present position but you also ensure that you will be able to expand into other EU markets in future years.

In addition, by having CTM scope you will add to the intrinsic value of your business. A brand that has exclusive rights in the 28 member states (and growing) will be more valuable than one that is exclusive to just one country.

Automatic extension

Any existing CTM will be automatically extended into any new EU entrant state, at no extra cost. That is, provided there is not already a conflicting mark on that member's national register.

National and CTM

The costs involved in both the national and CTM options are very modest. In both cases the period of cover is for an initial 10 years and is renewable.

Three for one

An added bonus with the CTM is that you can have three classes of goods or services registered for the same price as one class. (The EU is currently however considering introducing a separate fee for each class of goods or services). It is expected that the new

CTM law will not come into effective until the end of 2015, although this is not a fixed time frame.

Strategic move

Even if expansion into EU countries is not contemplated in the immediate future, one should seek registration in any field of activity where there is a possibility of use.

Additional classes

By covering these additional product/service classes in target markets, the business person gives himself the opportunity to get on with current matters while preserving future options. Moreover, by virtue of multi class fillings, in a market place as big as the EU, the intrinsic value of the original trade mark is enhanced.

It is vitally important that you protect your trade mark in your most important market. This is, in the majority of cases, your home country.

Even if you have no intention of exporting, either now or at some future date, do not postpone securing registration on the home front.

Protect home market

Many foreign companies avail of the CTM facility and so it is imperative that indigenous companies protect their trade mark interests by registering at least in their home market.

Burden of proof

Otherwise a rival with *the same or a confusingly similar identity* (where the overall impression given by the marks at issue is similar!) may obtain registration before the indigenous user. Then the burden of proof falls on the local company to prove, in a court of law, that its goodwill is being damaged by the new entrant.

Unregistered rights

This is an expensive and time-consuming exercise (that relies on common-law/unregistered rights) with no guarantee as to the outcome. The simple way to avoid possible lengthy litigation is to seek to register your trademark promptly.

Huge opportunities

By the same token if one moves speedily, and secures CTM registration, a plethora of possibilities await. Not only is one faced with a protective environment for personal expansion but also the prospects for franchise arrangements and licensing agreements are enhanced.

Increased value

A large proportion of the value of a company is based on its growth potential, which in turn is enhanced by its brands. It is also very true that brand valuation is therefore now beginning to confirm that brands are centrally important and enormously valuable corporate assets.

Goodwill and Loyalty

Brands create trust, goodwill and ultimately loyalty. It is the loyalty that delivers sustainable income to the company that owns the brands.

We have now covered the various considerations and steps associated with the subject-matter of trademark registration.

On the following two pages is a list of reminders when you

have chosen a mark to register.

Refer to them each time you are about to begin the process of trying to secure registration.

The following are the <u>critical points</u> in relation to trademarks.

1. Prior to use, it is essential to search the trade marks register in each target market. This will discover any existing names/marks that are the same, or confusingly similar, to that which is proposed and where the owner would have a sustainable objection to the new entrant.

2. If the search is clear, then an application should be made to register the mark in all markets where it is intended to use it.

3. Register in all classes of goods and services where it is currently used as well as in classes where there is intent to use. All goods and services are divided into 45 classes. It is advisable to gain exclusivity for the name in whichever classes one is intending to trade in the future. This will obviate the possibility of being frustrated at a later date.

4. The initial life of a registration is 10 years which can be renewed indefinitely each 10 years thereafter.

5. One can apply to register either nationally and/or seek a Community Trade Mark (CTM) registration.

The cost of an application, for each class, in Ireland, can be seen on www.patentsoffice.ie. At registration, approximately 6 months later, a further cost arises as detailed on the website.

6. A CTM registration provides exclusive rights to the mark in all member states of the European Union. With just one application, protection can be obtained in all countries of the EU. The cost of an application, which currently covers 3 classes of goods, can be seen on www.oami.europa.eu.

7. Additional classes are extra. When you have secured your CTM registration it is still incumbent on you, when entering a new market, to ensure that your mark does not infringe the existing rights of another trader in that market.

This ends the extracts from my first book,

"How to create your trade mark, protect it and build your brand" www.liammbirkett.com

Learn more from it too

If you found these few extracts informative and interesting, I urge you to read the book in its entirety.

It is full of advice, guidance and many stories and examples. These will further aid you in pursuit of your inventor scenario.

Strong and memorable

There you will read how to go about creating a suitable trade mark for your invention and build a brand for what it is you intend to market. Strong, memorable, protected identities that will make it jump off the shelves.

PLEASE NOTE

US differs from EU

Classification: unlike many EU states, the USPTO does not permit Nice class headings. The USPTO promotes the use of agreed terms. Applicants should check the ID MANUAL) the USPTO equivalent of OHIM's TMCLASS) for approved terms. If these are used the application should not then meet with any objections and this can save significant costs.

Actual use

Registration: if one has actual use or claims a foreign registration, a certificate of registration will issue at the end of the process. If it is an ITU basis, the mark will be allowed and the applicant then has 3 years to show actual use (by filing extensions of time every 6 months).

Maintenance

Renewal is every 10 years as in the EU. However, in the US, the holder must also prove actual use between the 5-6th years following registration (the "Section 8" Declaration). Any specified goods/services not then shown to be in use are simply cancelled.

Chapter 14: Answers To Your Test

Protected

You want to create a winner and you want to protect it. This shows you how to do just that.

Test time

Let's go back to the series of tasks set for you in chapter 3.

The first of these was to

Produce a toy with educational and artistic possibilities.

Have you come up with a solution that meets all the requirements you have read about? If not, take time out and try to crack it now.

The next few pages will tell you how one of these was invented and the important role branding played.

Story of UDRA

You come up with an idea that is simplicity itself. A jigsaw. It satisfies the inventive step requirement you learned about earlier in this book. It's a blank jigsaw.

Blank

No one ever had the idea of producing a blank jigsaw. Who, in Heaven's name, would want a blank jigsaw?

Search

Still, prompted by the advice earlier in this book (on Page 22) you do a "prior art" search.

Sure enough no one has ever filed a patent for a blank jigsaw.

So you decide to use the professional services of a patent attorney.

Create a trade mark

Meanwhile, you set about devising a trade mark to brand your product. You come up with a collection of letters – UDRA. Again, prompted by what you have learned in this book (Page 64) you undertake a search of the trade mark registers to see if your proposed trade mark is identical, or confusingly similar to an existing mark.

Cleared, you apply to register.

Gosh, you have learned a lot already from this book!

Robust patent

The patent attorney's initial reaction was very negative. How could one patent nothing? However, after much discussion, it was concluded that not only could it be the subject of a patent application, it would be a very robust patent. How could someone *nearly* infringe nothing?

List of benefits

Now, let's itemise the benefits of the invention. The jigsaw is made of white plastic material. It comes with some erasable felt tip markers. Using them, you can draw a map of a country and add in some cities, rivers, lakes, whatever picture you like.

Multi-use

Then you break up the jigsaw and let a friend/child try to re-assemble it. When it is complete, erase the drawing. Then use it to spell words, add up numbers and other tests, and repeat this routine as often as one wishes. Each time you do this you create a new challenge. That's inventive. It is non-obvious and so it is inventive.

Branding

Then turn to the trade mark. On the face of it, you have selected a random concoction of letters. Now combine them with the benefits of this jigsaw and the covert (hidden) reference becomes apparent. U D R A will be read to infer "You draw."

This has instant appeal to the marketing executive. What would a consumer expect to do with a 'you draw' jigsaw?

Patent and trade mark

Two important facts here: patent pending status and the trade mark registration process has begun.

You could easily have created both of these!

Overcoming rejection

Another story illustrates one of the important attributes an inventor should have – perseverance. The following is an extract from an article I wrote some years back that exemplifies this determination and a wonderful result.

Workmate

Back in 1968, an inventor, Ron Hickman, filed a patent for "A workbench".

At first he could not interest any company in his invention; in fact, Stanley Tools reckoned the product might sell in dozens rather than hundreds. Ron started to manufacture the workbench himself in his own garage and market it under the name WORKMATE (a name he rightly registered as a trade mark).

Black & Decker

Four years later Black & Decker agreed to manufacture and sales began to explode. Ron wrote a small book detailing his story in which he recounted Stanley Tools' observation. He was happy to point out that, at the time of writing, the 10 millionth WORKMATE had been sold!

That was in 1981 and, it is believed that, through various improvements to the workbench, patents are still in force to this day.

Your second challenge on Page 16

> *A travelling companion that ensures a neat appearance for trousers/slacks at all time.*

Executive companion

As you have noticed already identifying a regular problem is a great motivator to invention. It is well known that travelling executives like to maintain a neat appearance. Car or air journeys can play havoc with a pair of trousers. Rumpled legs don't project a well-dressed appearance.

Convenient size

Picture this, a small unit approx. X in length, Y in width and Z in thickness. This size sits neatly inside the bottom of a regular attaché case. There is still plenty of room for files, note books, calculator and the like.

Expandable

A neat travelling companion? When you take it from the case, it flips open to twice its length and the entire unit then hinges open. There is a mini heater element within the casing.

Open and closed case

The executive lays the front edge of the slacks along the opened base (just like on an ironing board) and sandwiches closed the two parts of the unit. These are held in place using in-built clamps. The unit is hung up by means of a hanger feature and an electrical lead from it is plugged into a socket in the house/hotel room. It is switched on and after 15 minutes an in-built timer clicks it off. The result is a perfectly pressed pair of trousers.

Clever branding

The name for this invention Razor's Edge describes the effect delivered without disclosing or describing the unit itself. A strong branding and ideal for trade mark registration.

YOU COULD HAVE DONE THAT!

Your next test

> *A thermometer that a child will readily allow into their mouth for long enough to get an accurate reading.*

Temperature reading

This is best explained by another true story. A parent who had to take a child's temperature regularly had great difficulty in getting the child to keep the thermometer in his mouth for any length of time.

Jingle

By chance, in his travels, the parent came across a birthday card which, when you opened it, played a happy birthday jingle. This prompted him to buy a few cards.

Legalese

Earlier we referred to the "known art" (something already known) and how this can negate the inventive step requirement.

Overcoming obstacles

Here is a different angle on this obstacle. It is possible to take two or more elements of known art and combine them – in an non-obvious way – to produce a new technical effect. (Sorry, had to introduce a little legalese here.)

In the present example

Reflect on this: a) the tune playing card was in the public domain and therefore part of the known art. For this reason you could not patent it. In fact, it might already be patented.

Likewise the thermometer is a known art. It too may be patented.

Opportunity

The clever parent saw, and seized a great opportunity. When he got home, he took the playing mechanism from the card and crudely attached it to the thermometer.

Distraction

He said to his child "Honey, you've got to leave this in your mouth until it stops playing." The child did just that. In fact the father had to play it again and again before the child would release it.

The parent had overcome a common problem in an non-obvious way.

He had taken two known arts and combined them in a way that satisfied the inventive step requirement.

He was able to apply for a patent.

He also came up with a name TEMPTUNE - a covert (hidden) reference to what the product does, which he could register as a trade mark TEMPTUNE.

YOU COULD HAVE DONE THAT!

Your next test

> *A way of keeping a spring-loaded door open without the use of weights, rope, hooks etc.*

Mind the gap

A door that stays open by magic (or so it seems). Have you cracked this task yet? The door must stay in an open position without the use of weights, hooks or, ropes.

Those skilled in the art cannot figure how this might be achieved. Consequently, the solution must be non-obvious and therefore, inventive.

Solution

Here's how to do it. Sink a magnetic disc into the door.

Put another into the adjoining wall at the same height as the one on the door. Now, when the door is opened to a certain position, the magnetic field will kick in and hold the door open (magically?).

YOU COULD HAVE DONE THAT!

Brand it

The trade mark for this invention could be found in the fairy-tale story of the hidden cave of treasures. The hero alone can gain entry by uttering the command "Open sesame". So why not market the SESAME door opener?

Simplicity

All of this goes to prove that simplicity is no barrier to invention. All of the foregoing required no huge expertise. No university degrees, technical qualifications or computer sciences were essential to the creation of these inventions or the devising of the trade marks.

I keep harking back to what I keep saying

YOU COULD HAVE DONE THAT!

YOU ARE AN INVENTOR

Mind set

However, you do need to get into the right mind set. Toss out all the negative thoughts that plague your mind. Jettison "I'm not good at this sort of thing."

This is the wrong mentality, one you must overcome.

Be positive, be determined, and take inspiration from the following little-known facts.

Ordinary people

Far too many of us believe that being creative is way outside of our capabilities and, to be an inventor, one must be an Einstein. This is far from the truth. A huge number of the best-known inventions were developed by people who came from different walks of life to the subject matter they created.

Different walks of life

It would be fair to assume that an engineer invented the ballpoint pen but, in fact, the idea was developed by a Hungarian hypnotist.

Odd collection

Equally surprising are the inventors of the following list: Frisbee, a building inspector; Monopoly, a heating engineer; Photocopier, a land-claim official; Brillo, a manufacturer of costume jewellery and the Telephone Answering Machine, an American businessman!

You can too

If these people can do it, so can you. Every day in manufacturing, for instance, people come up with novel ways to get the job done. Often, this is merely to overcome an obstacle, get the product out on time, and rush on to the next task. The same applies in all walks of life from farming to services.

Problem solving

Something is put together to solve a problem, whether that be using a piece of farm machinery or an implement in an unusual way, coming up with a new way of fixing a garden hose or stopping a pot from boiling over on the cooker.

If these innovations are of use and solve a known, regular problem, they are of interest to others who encounter similar difficulties. This makes them marketable.

If they are not patentable, what then?

There are a variety of options that can be used to protect your innovation. We will itemise them now and evaluate their robustness.

Chapter 15: Design Rights

Registered design protection

There are two alternatives for you to consider. The first is to seek registered design protection. You can apply for a National and/or Registered Community Design (RCD) before you market your product.

Up to 25 years

This form of protection is initially valid for five years from the date of filing and can be renewed in blocks of five years up to a maximum of 25 years.

Unregistered design protection

Alternatively, you may opt to begin marketing your product, without applying to register it and rely on what is known as the Unregistered Community Design (UCD) right.

Only for 3 years

This form of protection is given for a period of three years from the date on which the design was first made available to the public within the European Union. After three years, the protection cannot be extended. The criteria for unregistered design rights are the same as for registered design right, i.e. it must be novel and have individual character.

One year grace period

In the event that you change your mind, after you have disclosed your design, and want to apply for a design registration you can still do so. Within one year of disclosure, you have what's known as the 'grace period' to apply for registration. If you register your design after that, it will be vulnerable to attack.

Registered design

You can get exclusive rights to a product your design if it is a new or original design. This refers to the shape and configuration of the finished article. Anything that is new, but contained within an item and therefore not visible to the naked eye, is not capable of registration. Almost any industrial or handicraft item can be eligible for design protection

Definition

A 'product' is defined as 'any industrial or handicraft item'. A design is considered to have an individual character if the overall impression it produces differs significantly from existing designs. The protection also covers the ornamentation that may embellish the surface of the item.

Legal wording

The protection covers 'the appearance of the whole or a part of a product resulting from the features of, in particular, the lines, contours, colours, shape, texture and/or materials of the product itself and/or its ornamentation'.

Non-disclosure

Subject to the 1 year grace period, the product must not be put on public display prior to application for registration. If the product is available to the public before you apply for registration, it can jeopardise your ability to register it as a design. (There are certain exceptions in relation to exhibitions and works shown in confidence). The act of making the product available to the public is called 'disclosure'.

Duration

The initial duration is for a period of five years and can be renewed twice more up to a total of 15 years. It is often the case, because designs are so transient, that a Mark 11 and Mark 111 will emerge and the updated versions will be applied for registration in favour of staying with the original design. However, the changes themselves must have individual character.

CTM and RCD

There was a time when we had to go country by country to apply to register intellectual property rights. However, this changed with the arrival of the EU's Community Trade Mark (CTM). What started out as embracing only 12 countries have grown to 28 now, with more to follow.

National or Community-wide

The same situation is mirrored in the Registered Community Design (RCD). You may wish to apply to register your design in only one country (perhaps your own national filing). However, with only one application to the Office for Harmonisation of the Internal Market (OHIM) you can register your design in all 28 member states.

Added benefits

If your idea/invention is not patentable, there are other avenues to explore. You can, as we have stated, still enjoy a level of protection for it in the design of your product. This could, for example, have been the case, in respect of the Razor's Edge. The exclusivity would have been in the overall appearance of the finished product (as well as registering the trade mark.)

Variations

In your filing, you can include a number of variations to the design and configuration of your product. Potential rivals would have to go outside the scope of these representations to avoid infringing your rights.

Ornamentation

In addition to this defensive mode there is also another protective layer. Not only is the shape protected but also is its ornamentation. For example we could have a repeat pattern of the Razor's Edge logotype, or its symbol, incorporated in the panels of the unit.

Imitations spotted

This makes for very strong consumer recognition.

Any possible me-too imitation would be easily spotted by the consumer as not being the genuine article.

Be vigilant

However, it is important that you play a part in protecting you rights. You have to ensure that nobody uses your design in the marketplace. You can do this by keeping an eye on newspapers, magazines and trade publications. Look too at the Internet and for companies that are using your design without your permission.

Illegal copies

You may spot illegal copies of your products on sale. These can be from competitors who are using designs that are even similar, although not identical, to your registered design. In both cases you are entitled to enforce your rights.

Seizures

You can also take advantage of a customs monitoring service provided by your national customs authority. If customs officers, come across potentially infringing products (using a database in which all applications are centralised) they can seize the infringing goods.

Relatively inexpensive

Given the number of countries and the scope of protection, a RCD is very good value. Here are some details of official fees.

Online application for a Community design from €350

Registration €230

Additional registration

2 to 10 = €115

11 = €50

The fees payable depend on whether the application contains one or more designs

The fee structure

There is a basic fee for a single design or the first design of a multiple application. The fee is reduced for the 2nd to 10th designs. There is a further fee reduction per design, from the 11th design onwards

Marketing mix

With the protection garnered and the relatively small outlay, the RCD is worth considering in your overall marketing mix.

Chapter 16: Copyright

Other means of protection

Although registration is the best and strongest way to protect your trade mark, certain aspects of branding may be protected by other means, even in the absence of (or perhaps pending) trade mark registration.

Copyright-unregistered right

One of these is copyright. It is an unregistered right. This means you don't have to file it anywhere and pay a fee. Moreover, it lasts for your lifetime and 70 years after you pass away. It comes into play in many scenarios. More particularly, copyright can provide protection for any original literary, dramatic, musical or artistic work, computer programme or database.

Artistic input

There can be copyright in the artistic work of the drawings of one's invention, an innovative product and even the design of the logotype of the brand name or symbolism.

Copyright – how it affects you

It is important that you have some knowledge of what copyright is and the scope and protection it offers. There are few who do not produce something that falls within this gambit- writers, artists, designers, musicians, techies etc.

Everyone should be aware

Employers, employees, free lancers and consultants should

understand their rights in their various areas of business and endeavours. Copyright subsists, that is, it exists, and protects certain forms of original work.

Scope

It is worth setting out to what copyright relates. Copyright protection extends to any original literary, dramatic musical or artistic works; sound recordings, films, broadcasts or cable programmes; typographical arrangements of published editions and databases.

New rights

For copyright protection to exist, the work must be recorded in writing or other tangible form (e.g. sound recording or film). Copyright shall not subsist in a work which infringes copyright in another work. There are rental and lending rights for authors, while satellite broadcasting and cable transmissions are also covered.

Details

For the effort, imagination and skill put into the creative outputs listed above, it is said that copyright subsists.

International

Copyright is an international protection no matter where or by whom the work is created. Moreover there are no costs involved. It is provident, although not essential, for the *author* of the work to attach ©, the year, and his/her name at the bottom of the work. During the author's lifetime and for 70 years after their demise,

no one can legally copy the relevant work to a material or substantial extent. It is the judge who ultimately decides what is *substantial* and that varies on the nature of the copied works.

Witness

If a third party does copy the work, there can be copyright infringement. So, for reasons of evidence, it is worth getting a reputable person to witness and date your original work. This applies to such things as a song, painting, story, web page or computer programme. No one can legally copy and/or use this work, to a material or substantial extent, without the author's permission.

Now, back to definitions

"Author" is defined as the person who creates the work (for sound recordings, the 'author' is the producer; for film, it is the producer and principal director; for photographs, it is the photographer; and so on). The list is extensive and has a number of features. For instance the owner of copyright in a photograph used to be the person who owned the material on which the photograph was taken – now it is the person who takes the picture.

Moral rights

Authors can object to distortion, mutilation or other modification of, or other derogatory action, in relation to their works that would prejudice their reputation.

Who owns what?

By way of example, a photographer now also has the (paternity) right to be identified as the author and the (integrity) right to object to any derogatory use or treatment of the photograph. A person commissioning a photograph, although the photographer holds the copyright, has a (privacy) right to object to the photograph being made available to the public.

Employer/employee

There are some interesting exceptions. For example, copyright on work produced by an employee in the course of employment is owned by the employer unless otherwise agreed. In the case of newspapers and periodicals, the employee may be free to use the work for purposes other than use in those media.

Contractors

An employer is the owner of copyright in a work created by an employee in the course of his/her employment. Contractors are different; they are the first owners of copyright. Always ensure there is explicit advance agreement in writing to obviate any confusion that might arise at a later date.

Commissioned works

It is also worth highlighting the fact that copyright in commissioned works belongs to the author unless they specifically assign the copyright to someone else (such as the person who commissioned the work).

Other recordings

As was said earlier, in most countries, the duration of copyright is generally 70 years after the death of the author. This refers to original literary, artistic, musical and dramatic works, sound and music recordings, and films. For broadcasts, the total length of the copyright is 50 years and for typographical arrangements, 25 years.

Much power

However, the owner of the copyright has much more power over the work with regards to copying, storing, photographing, broadcasting, adapting, renting or lending the work. Moreover, an infringer now can be the person who facilitates the infringement, by way of import, export, sale, rental, loan or otherwise (such as people who sell bootleg copies of films or CDs, or websites that enable people to illegally download films).

Fines and imprisonment

Some of the restricted acts relate to rights and legal ramifications in Irish law. In Ireland, an existing Act criminalises infringement of Intellectual Property rights and provides for very heavy fines and terms of imprisonment. This should be very effective as a deterrent to those who might consider infringing the rights of others and give substantial recompense to anyone infringed.

Exemplary damages

The Irish Courts may, in addition or as an alternative to awarding compensation for financial loss to the injured party, impose aggravated and/or exemplary damages. Any person who breaks the law is liable on summary conviction (that is trial without a jury) to a very hefty fine in respect of **each** infringing copy or to imprisonment for up to 12 months, or both. Where there is conviction on indictment (trial by jury) the fine goes up dramatically and imprisonment can be for up to 5 years, or both.

Strong intent

The Irish Government has given very high priority to the issue of intellectual property. The Government has stated that it will continue to do so to ensure that the country keeps pace with societal and technological changes and international developments.

Chapter 17: A Cautionary Tale

You may think that it is impossible to infringe a copyright of "nothing". However, it has happened.

SILENCE IS STOLEN

When you create a most unusual musical work the last thing that you want to happen is to be ripped off. When the artistic composition consists of the absence of sound there would seem little likelihood that this could happen. But that is exactly what has occurred some years ago in the U.K.

Fatal error

The alleged guilty party was British composer Mike Batt. While working with a classical group known as the Planets in producing a CD comprised of variations of several well-known pieces, he made a fatal error.

Just a minute

In memory and appreciation of a then deceased composer, John Cage, he added a final track of, yes, you've guessed it, *silence*. He highlighted this accreditation on the album sleeve by listing the composer of the one-minute track as "Batt/Cage".

This has incurred the wrath of the Cage estate.

Four minutes 33 seconds

In 1952 John Cage had created considerable notoriety for himself by composing a musical work consisting of four minutes thirty-three seconds of silence. This was premiered at an almost open-air venue at Woodstock, New York, by a pianist during an avant-garde charity function. The audience sat bemused while the performer put the hand-written score on the music stand of the piano. He then closed the lid and sat stationary with stopwatch in hand while he counted down the length of the silent movement.

Nature's sound

He raised and lowered the lid of the piano to indicate the beginning and end of each movement, the total amounting to 4' 33''. The only sounds were those of the trees rustling in the breeze and, at another point, the patter of rain! In other words, the sound of nature and the environment.

Infringement

By encroaching on this silent composition, the Batt minute was said to have infringed the copyright in the Cage's original work.

Mother's pride

Probably the most telling comment came from Batt's mammy when she said, "Which part of the silence are they claiming you nicked?" To infringe copyright one has to copy all, or a substantial part of, the earlier work. Could 60 seconds be considered to be a substantial part of 273 seconds … of silence?

Nice gesture

The case settled later, without going to court, by an ex gratia payment of a reputedly £100,000 donated by Mr Batt.

Chapter 18: Copyright vs Trade Mark

Logotypes

Copyright protection may apply to some brand elements. Probably the most obvious of these is a logotype. That is the distinctive way in which a trade mark is designed. A classic example is the famous Coca Cola logo. Such an element may be protected because it can be judged to be an original work of art.

Jingles, Slogans and taglines

Other aspects of a brand may also enjoy copyright protection, such as musical jingles (if it is an original musical work). So too, potentially, can a slogan or tagline (it being considered as an original literary work).

Automatic, international and free

Copyright arises automatically upon creation of a protectable work. As a result, it is free and does not need to be registered and the protection extends internationally. That said, it is important to recognise that copyright only protects against actual copying. In many cases, it may be difficult and expensive to prove that a competitor has copied your copyrighted brand features. If that work is created independently, it is not an infringement of your copyright.

Prove its existence

Moreover, because copyright is not registered, in the event of a dispute, it is necessary to prove both that copyright subsists (that means it exists) in the infringed mark and you demonstrate ownership of the protected matter.

No longer than 70 years

Although most businesses are more concerned with the present
and near future rather than the long term, it is worth remembering
also that copyright expires 70 years after the demise of the author
of the copyrighted work.

Trade marks can be protected forever

In contrast, a registered trade mark can be protected in perpetuity
if it is put to proper use and is renewed every ten years. In
summary, then, logos and possibly also other brand elements, may
automatically enjoy some level of protection under copyright even
if those features are not the subject of trade mark registration.

Limitations

However, the limitations of, and challenges in enforcing
copyright, mean that it is almost always advisable to register your
trade marks rather than merely relying on copyright protection.

Summary

In summary, then, logos and other brand elements can
automatically enjoy some level of protection under copyright,
even if those features are not the subject of trade mark registration.

Good advice

While it is not essential, it is advisable to attach © the year of
creation of the work (this could be the design sketch of your
invention for instance) and your name to the work in question.
This puts others on notice that you know your rights and are likely
to enforce them.

Intellectual property rights

A more detailed version can be used where it is appropriate and space allows e.g.

Chapter 19: A Quick Review

It's time to pause and recap on what you have learned. You now know:

1. What is inventive and what is not

2. The three essentials for a patent

3. About subject matter searching

4. How to draft a patent specification

5. How to file a patent application

6. The priority period for further filing

7. How to take advantage of patent pending status

8. How to create a good trade mark

9. How to file for a trade mark

10. How to use TM and ®

11. The benefits of a Community Trade Mark (CTM)

12. To "be first and brand it"

13. How to use national design rights

14. When to use unregistered design rights

15. About Registered Community Design (RCD)

16. Your idea does not have to be patentable

17. Your idea should address a need or provide a benefit

18. You don't need academic qualifications

19. You don't need any technical expertise

Away you go

Armed with all this know-how, examples and stories you must by now realise and accept that you are an inventor.

Invention is not beyond your capabilities. You are someone who can turn a clever idea into a commercial success. You have a clearly defined road map to follow.

Lots more to inspire and help you

Chapter 20: Bringing Inventiveness To The Surface

Over the years, I have written many articles that illustrate how inventiveness came to the surface. They demonstrate how inventors showed their brilliance, coupled with their determination and spirit to succeed.

Look behind the stories and find the hidden secrets to guide you on your way to success.

An eye opener

Everyone is aware of the cat's eyes that run down the centre of the roads. They probably believe that the innovation was patented by someone for the *eyes element* alone.

Not so

This is not the case. It was in 1934 that a UK inventor, Percy Shaw, patented the idea of cats-eyes as an improvement to road markings, the first cat's eyes were installed in the north of England but went on to improve safety on a world-wide basis.

More to it than that

The patent did not relate to simply the placing of eyes on the road, it was more complicated, and therefore more likely to be the subject matter of a patent, than that. Mr Shaw foresaw that if the eyes were sitting in the middle of the road then, in no time at all, they would be covered in dirt and grime thrown up by passing traffic.

Housing

He then designed a rubber-housing unit for the eyes that could be half-sunk into the roadway. The housing would also incorporate a spring that sat between the eyes holding up the top layer of the rubber covering that ran across the upmost part of the unit. Then, when vehicles ran over the housing, the eyes were forced down and "blinked" themselves clean. Therein lay the ingenuity, and, the inventiveness.

That's not yours, it's mine.

There have been some developments in the field of inventions that have raised not only eyebrows, but also the question of who owns what. If you invent something, then you should enjoy the rewards that go with the successful exploitation of your ingenuity, right? Wrong! Well, maybe not. Much depends on where you live and work.

Thorny question (From years ago)

All hell broke loose in Japan and focussed attention once more on the thorny question of ownership of patented inventions in many parts of the world.

Easily LED

In 2004, the man who invented the blue light-emitting diode (LED) that we are all familiar with and who was employed by the Nichia Corporation in Japan won 20 billion yen from his former employer. The position in respect of intellectual property rights (IPR) in that country is that the employee can retain the patent rights for something he invents.

Reasonable compensation

In Japan employees can retain the patent rights for something they invent. To transfer the Intellectual Property Rights to the company, the employer must ensure that the inventor is reasonably compensated. And herein lays the rub. What exactly does this mean and how it is quantified? Historically, it was the company supremoes who decided on the recompense to the inventor. Now, the inventive employees are rebelling against this system and suing for what they consider just rewards.

Be reasonable

Because there is not a precise definition, in Japanese law, of what is meant by "reasonably compensated", cases are going before the courts to seek clarification.

Pay out

Hitachi was ordered to pay 162 million yen to the inventor of its optical disc reader, while a food company, Ajinomoto had to pay almost 200 million yen to the person who created the huge selling artificial sweetener it markets. By comparison, the Nichia award of 20 billion puts these somewhat in the shade.

Follow that

Encouraged by these favourable decisions and pay-outs, it is reasonable to expect that current, and past, inventive employees will more closely scrutinise their remuneration packages. If the tide turned in Japan, there is a likelihood that something similar can occur on this side of the world.

Not in the UK

However, in the UK the law favours the employer. There, the patent rights automatically reside, not with the employee who invents something in the course of his work, but with his employer. (The employee does have a right to compensation in the event the company enjoys an outstanding benefit arising from the invention.)

Change coming?

When inventors learn of the rewards being obtained by their counterparts overseas this acceptance may be disturbed. It might motivate some to seek change.

Know your rights

In any event, these developments should spur all parties to review the status quo. Have employers taken steps to familiarise themselves with the law as it relates to them? Have they got appropriate employment contracts in place? Do they adequately promote and reward an ethos of invention?

University challenge

What if someone in such an institution is working on a project that might result in an application for a patent? Does an individual, student, lecturer, team or the college authorities have claim to the patent?

Written agreement

In some instances, provident steps have been taken and the matter has been addressed by way of written agreement or contract at the commencement of the project or term. Then each party knows exactly what has been agreed. In the absence of this problems can arise.

Hell to pay

A rule of thumb that has been applied is that if one is in an employment relationship (to lecture, teach, instruct) the rights reside with the institution. If however, you are not being paid (say, you are a student) you may have some rights to a resulting patent, provided the college does not have a clause in its policy that it owns the Intellectual Property created by its students. Check it out!

Change of Direction

Almost every existing or aspiring inventor hopes to patent their invention in the United States. The size, purchasing power and consumers' almost insatiable appetite for anything novel makes it a prime target. The examining bodies that grant patents in either Europe or the US have differed on a number of issues in the past and are not without divergences at present.

More accepting

Driven, mainly by the powers-that-be across the Atlantic, (who say almost anything can be patented) their counterparts over here are now accepting applications for patents on subject matter that was previously taboo. The patent offices in each jurisdiction have different requirements in drafting patent specifications but experienced patent attorneys are well-versed in these nuances.

Different drafting

However, recent decisions from the US courts have suggested a restrictive view on patentability. We await further decisions from the US courts to see how this interesting topic evolves.

DYSON BLOWS UP A STORM OF CONTRVERSY AND WINS (Another story from the archives)

James Dyson's Cyclone domestic appliance fills a vacuum the opposition cannot fill.

Many years ago the UK High Court handed down a decision that was of great interest to inventors everywhere. It carried many of the hallmarks of the old David versus Goliath story albeit that by now David has grown pretty strong himself. At the time the *youth* in question was James Dyson (whose company matured into one of the top 100 unquoted companies with a high profit growth rates in the UK) and his then Nemesis, none other than the mighty, multi-national corporation, Hoover.

Offered to others

In those days of yore, when Dyson first invented his revolutionary method of collecting dust and perfected his bag-less vacuum cleaner he, rather than go into manufacturing himself, offered his technology to existing manufacturers. At that time none of them showed any interest.

Money bags

He has suggested that part of the reason for the negative response was their reluctance to miss out on the highly remunerative bag replacement business which netted them millions of sales each year.

Creating a cyclone

So, rather than let his 15 years of research and development lie fallow and with a hell-bent desire to see his invention on the market, James decided to make the cleaners himself. The inspiration for his invention was to come up with something which would overcome what he perceived as a major drawback on the existing regular form of vacuum cleaner.

Lack of suction

He saw bags as being not only messy and wasteful but also, as they filled with the dust being sucked up, cut down on the power of the suction itself. His aim was to eliminate the bag and to do this he created the "Cyclone" a vacuum cleaner that would not lose suction.

100 patent applications

This new methodology he protected with patents and ever since then continued to protect it as each new improvement ensued.

Media exposure

Because of his powers of self-promotion and not hindered by his good looks and affable manner the story of his subsequent success will be well known to most. Regular press coverage and radio/TV interviews (at the time this article was written) succeeded in making his a recognisable face and his "Dual Cyclone" a highly sought after product and a trade mark exclusively his throughout the European Union.

Award of Court

In his judgement, Mr Justice Michael Fysh held that Hoover's "Triple Vortex" did infringe the scope of Dyson's patents. The essence of the case rested on the use of centrifugal force used to separate the dust from the air being sucked into the cleaner and storing it in a compartment rather than a replaceable bag.

Growing success

In 2015 Dyson employs more than 4,000 people around the world and holds over 3,000 patents.

Does that taste funny or am I crackers?

When it comes to branding the scenario has been greatly expanded as to what can be registered as a trade mark and, consequently, enjoy statutory protection. One of the most novel forms, and seldom used, is taste.

Good taste

Yes, it is possible to register a taste as a trade mark. Therefore, it awaits the creativity of some marketing person to come up with a possible registration and so steal a march on the rest of us and gain the attendant publicity that will undoubtedly go with it.

Chew on this

An example would be producing packaging for say, toothpaste, which if bitten into would taste of spearmint. Or perhaps rice paper which, when chewed, would have a sweet and sour taste or curry from an envelope that carries recipes for Indian food. The imagination need only be challenged before some clever uses will emerge.

At the forefront

Those fortunate to be at the forefront will reap the publicity rewards. Eli Lilly & Co was the first to apply for a Community Trade Mark (CTM). This company sought to register an *artificial strawberry flavour* in respect of packaging for pharmaceutical preparations.

Smell of success

If you are piped to the post in this country don't lose heart it is also possible to apply to register shapes, sounds and even smells as trade marks. Applications have been made in respect of roses for automobile tyres and the smell of stale beer for the flights on darts. So the opportunity is there to be grasped.

Confucius, he say...

Chinese restaurants the world over have an added feature to their eating experience which seems to be uniquely theirs. Only in these establishments are diners treated to free fortune cookies at the end of the meal. Great enjoyment and fun can be had from eating these tasty morsels and sharing with friends the secret messages they hold. It is interesting to reflect on how the cookies are made and from where the sage messages originate.

Patented method

Perhaps it is not surprising to learn that the methodology that forms the unusual shape was patented. Yongsik Lee patented the fortune cookie machine that incorporates a number of griddles on which the cookie blanks are placed and then passed through an oven where they are baked. There is then a transfer mechanism that slides the baked cookie onto a second unit for the depositing of a message on each one and folding them. The cookies are then allowed to cool.

Patented machines

Mr Lee began selling his patented machines to a multitude of bakers and became the biggest seller in the United States. His success brought with it some unexpected headaches.

Interesting snippets

These people needed an almost endless supply of "fortune" telling strips, for insertion into the cookies they produced, to entertain the readers. Lee started to build up a stock of fortunes the majority of them culled from anything from religious manuscripts to Almanacs.

Although everyone should take these "pearls of wisdom" with a grain of salt and as a bit of fun as they are intended, amazingly, some can take exception to the message.

New opportunity

In time this spawned a new industry whereby not only are people specially commissioned to create new messages that will be universally acceptable but also the demand seems to be endless. Submissions come from contributors from all walks of life, students, teachers, free-lance writers, all of whom contribute differing themes.

Because of the need to be cost efficient at every stage of the process, while the cookies themselves are the biggest part of the costs, more ingenuity is required. The messages have to be paid for, printed, guillotined, packed, dispatched and still show a profit. No easy challenge.

New entrepreneur

Here again, it appears that one source, a sort of one-man-Chinese-born-band, Steven Yang, has cornered a big chunk of this market. He churns out millions of messages to feed the insatiable appetite for such fortunes.

Inspiration for you

There are a number of challenges on offer. Why not develop a new patentable way of producing something kindred to the cookie? If the original cookies sell into Chinese restaurants taking this simple concept and giving it broader appeal could broaden the market.

Ditto for other outlets

You could come up with something that would work in all restaurants, coffee bars, pubs and even shops. The consumer might like to read an inspiring message at any of these locations and also buy a supply for entertaining at home.

Patent potential

Either way, if a patent is obtained exclusivity may be enjoyed for a period of 20 years, the lifetime of a patent. Maybe then you won't have to seek your fortune in a fortune cookie. If all else fails, try writing a million fortunes, Mr Yang needs all the messages he can get.

Something along the same lines

Christmas Crackers - what an oversight!

It's no joke when it comes to Christmas Crackers. Probably the corniest one-liners are to be found inside them not to mention the comical paper hats and *invaluable* trinkets. But would we be without them? Never. What would the festive dinner table be without those colourful additions?

Who started it?

We now take them for granted but do you know how they came into being and how the originator missed out on having the marketing bonanza to himself?

New concept

It all began back in 1847 when a young man who had started out in a confectionery shop in London went on to make the most of his experiences and innovative skills. Tom Smith was a hard-working, creative lad who was forever dreaming up new concepts and designs for the ornaments and decorations that were sold for the cakes his employer baked.

New venture

His efforts were rewarded when he was bold enough to go into business for himself and began marketing sugared almond sweets wrapped in tissue paper.

Little mottos

In an effort to stimulate sales during slow periods Tom hit on the idea of putting little mottoes, mainly of the romantic variety, printed on paper, inside the wrappers of his offerings. This turned out to be an inspired ploy and his business prospered.

Christmas crackers

It is said that it was while he was sitting in front of a blazing log fire enjoying its heat and listening to the crackle of the wood that the seeds of what was to become his Christmas cracker were born.

Following a great deal of experimenting he eventually came up with the correct formulation of *explosive* and friction to provide the bang we hear today. This strip he combined with his motto slip, added a small gift, and wrapped them in colourful paper. The cracker had arrived. It proved to be an almost instant success.

Patent miss

Alas and alack poor Tom never explored the possibility of seeking a patent for his invention and so the possibility of exclusivity in his chosen markets was lost. And from being the sole manufacturer of crackers, with excellent sales in the UK and wonderful prospects for sales overseas, the inevitable happened.

Copycats

Once his products were seen abroad Eastern companies were quick to jump on the bandwagon and began producing copycat crackers. To add insult to industry they exported them to the UK.

If a patent had been obtained then the world could have been his oyster at least for 20 years, the lifetime of a patent.

Sole right

Anywhere a patent is held, no one can legally manufacture or sell the patented product without the permission of the patent holder. So Tom Smith could have decided to be the sole manufacturer and exporter or granted licences to third parties. Either way the potential was explosive.

Put a price on 'new' and exploit it

A whole new series of metrics appear by which businesses are valued and judged. These have turned conventional wisdom on its head. Now, some of the most sought after shares are those of companies that have lost, and continue to lose, millions of dollars every month from inception. Many of these concerns have no tangible properties such as buildings and transport they are purely *clicks and mortar.*

Amazon

The catalyst for this change has been the internet. A classic example being Amazon.com which now offers for sale almost anything under the sun via the World Wide Web.

100 years ago

But the past holds many examples of how innovation radically changed how we perceive and utilise that which surrounds us. In so doing fortunes have been made by those who saw that their time had come and reacted promptly. Let's go back 100 years.

Light up

Thomas Edison, inventor of the electric light bulb, experimented with electricity for many years before the introduction of his product. He bided his time until the critical mass of urbanisation justified the investment of resources and provided the consumer market on which to capitalise.

The greatest thing

A jeweller, Otto Rohwedder, in the early days of the 1900s, was a man who was fascinated with the concept of having a sliced pan. His efforts and idea was of little avail until 1925 and the introduction of a bread wrapping machine. He filed for a patent in 1928 and within a few years 80% of bread sold in the United States was pre-sliced. However poor old Otto died in 1960 without realising a fortune.

Tea bags

In 1904, New Yorker, Thomas Sullivan (he's got to have Irish connections) to save money on the tin boxes needed to send out his tea samples, used tiny silk sacks instead. His customers (probably not Irish) put these bags into the tea pot and, unwittingly, invented the tea bag!

Good tip

A secretary, in an effort to cover up her typing errors, took to using a tab of white paint. With a little help from her friends she perfected this somewhat and marketed it as *Liquid Paper*, selling it in some 30 countries. In the late 1900s she sold out to Gillette and was worth more than $50 million. She continued collecting a royalty on every bottle sold world-wide. Her young son, Michael, who had helped her in the beginning also made a name for himself as a monkey in the Monkees pop group.

Snap decision

Edwin Land was born in 1909 and went on to invent the *Polaroid* camera which was launched for sale in 1948. His product was unrivalled until Kodak introduced their version in 1976. They ran into legal problems and, $1 billion in damages later, withdrew from the marketplace in 1985.

Small is beautiful

Three researchers at Bell Laboratories on December 23 1947 created the nascent semiconductor which could deliver signal messages in milliseconds. These became transistors which grew smaller and more capable of performing amazing feats. The electronic age was upon us!

Billionaires

All of the above, and more, has made this millennium's plateau possible. It has enabled Billionaires to be the legal tender that surpasses and minimises millionaires in the lexicon of modern business parlance.

Entrepreneurial spirit

The common denominator throughout has been the entrepreneurial spirit, the recognition to patent inventions and brand them, then reap the rewards. Nothing has really changed except the size of the rewards - for all of us who enjoy the payback or the facilities.

Now it's your turn

Now, it is your turn. The Internet is your medium. You can afford to reach untold millions of consumers world-wide, in their language of choice, and at their local time, as never was before is within your capability.

Start up success

No longer do you have to be so many years in business, have such and such a track record of recorded profit growth and boast a staff of big numbers. These criteria have been paralleled with new ones, exploit them to the full. Make this millennium your window of opportunity.

Gun Battle, who is firing at whom?

Mention the word Kalashnikov to anyone and the first thing that pops into his or her mind is "rifle". The infamous AK- 47 is a weapon familiar to most of us who read the papers or listen to the radio when there is reporting from the war torn areas around the world or even closer to home.

Surname

Few may know that this is the surname of the inventor, Mikhail Timofeevich Kalashnikov, who was a much-decorated officer in the Russian Army. Moreover, his weapon has been the subject of a long fought war between Russian companies over the intellectual property rights in relation to his invention.

Anomalies

The details of the dispute are still vague and the reporting, at best, is very hit and miss. It appears that the protection that might be available under copyright law is being confused with that of patent protection. In both respects, there are anomalies that need to be examined and resolved.

Inspiration

But let's start with a bit about the man himself. It was while he was recovering in hospital from war battle wounds sustained during the Second World War that tank commander Kalashnikov turned his mind to conceiving a machine gun that would be simple to make, light in weight yet heavy in fire power. He produced the first prototype in 1944 and five years later the Soviet army had it as their standard rifle.

Licenced

The Soviets kept the AK-47 under wraps throughout the Second World War and soldiers were instructed to keep the rifles hidden in pouches. After that manufacturing rights (licences) were granted to satellite countries such as Bulgaria and the Czech Republic.

Non payment

The reported court case referred to 19 countries in which the gun is manufactured, few of which have been paying royalties. It is difficult to determine how exactly intellectual property rights could now attach to the rifle. The lifetime of a patent is 20 years and, unless there were a number of radical innovative improvements to it, which could have extended the period of cover, then any protection obtained in the '40s has long since expired.

Contractual restrictions

Copyright lasts for the lifetime of the author of a work and 70 years of his demise, so that could still apply, if it was applicable. But is it? If original drawings, mouldings and/or tooling were provided to bona fide licensees in some instances then these may still be subject to contractual restrictions. Perhaps some availed of these but reneged on paying royalties and hence the reported legal dispute?

Bad Lands

However, when one looks to the obvious suspect countries where these guns of destruction are hammered out in workshops in the mountainous Bad Lands it is difficult to see how any IP rights can be infringed, never mind enforced!

Trade mark potential

One other point to be examined is that of trade mark violation. Were the names Kalashnikov or AK - 47 ever sought to be registered and if so in what countries? It appears that neither Kalashnikov nor AK-47 can no longer, if they ever could, fulfil the basic requirements of a valid trade mark. That is to identify the origin of the product. Their use in the West is recognised as being, in the generic sense, as relating to "that kind of gun".

Other products

It will be interesting to learn, in time, the further details of this dispute. Clever marketers in the West might have been opportunistic by, for instance, coming out with a laxative or alcoholic drink branded with either of the two names. We might have seen advertising that read "Kalashnivok, the drink that knocks 'em dead" or "Experience Heaven, have an AK-47". Meanwhile one might speculate that the story from Russia is a bit half-cocked.

Crossfire

While on the topic of guns, there are two other stories that are sometimes confusingly interlinked. These refer to the infamous Chicago bank robber of the '30s, Henry Dillinger and Henry Deringer. The former found his way into American folklore when he escaped from jail using a small gun that is alternatively said to have been fashioned out of soap then coloured with boot polish, made of wood or smuggled in by a friend.

Wrong title

Whatever the real story, a number of "genuine" originals are on exhibit in various museums in the United States. Dillinger is sometimes incorrectly used to describe a small gun that is easily concealed on one's person. It should be referred to as Deringer for the following reason.

Crack shot inventor

Henry Deringer of Philadelphia invented and marketed a single shot pocket pistol in 1830. It rapidly became very popular because of its ease of concealment and was the gun used in the assassination of Abraham Lincoln. Unfortunately, because of its widespread use and effectiveness the Deringer name began to be used in the generic sense and was applied to the many imitations that began to emerge.

Look a likes

Henry then sued to obtain sole use of the name for his own range of pistols. In an ill-conceived effort to avoid infringement gun manufacturers such as Colt and Remington referred to their look-a-likes as "derringer", using the double "r" to avoid confusion.

Get your registration

It is easy to see how all these names get jumbled in the minds of storytellers. However, bring it right up to date it highlights the importance of branding; choosing a good, memorable trade mark, clearing it for use and the registering it so that no one can legally have an identical or confusingly similar mark.

Gun ho

Strange, that at the same time as one famous "gun man" makes the headlines another features for a completely different set of reasons. Hot on the heels of inventor Kalashnikov, the inventor of another machine gun, the UZI, appears in the obituary listings.

Huge sales

Uzi Gal, died at the age of 79. It was he who gave his name to name to the rapid shooting firearm that has recorded sales in excess of $2bn since its introduction half a century ago.

Objection denied

Unlike the Russian army general whose name made headlines because of alleged copyright infringement associated with the AK47, Mr Gal never wanted his moniker to identify his invention. In fact he tried to stop such branding but his objection was denied by the Israeli Military Industries, the concern that manufactures the gun.

Movie star

It gained Hollywood status when, in the movie, *The Terminator,* the alien being, played by Arnold Schwarzenegger toted this weapon of destruction as he/it made its way among mere humans.

First hoardings

Around 1850 a young man from the East End of London was quick to see the media potential presented by the introduction of new railways. He began renting from landlords' vacant sites along the lines for a few shillings. On these he erected advertising spaces which he in turn rented to advertisers at a considerable profit. The first users of these were manufacturers of patent medicines. The clever entrepreneur gave his name to the new medium, he was Samuel Hoarding.

Lit up

An advertising agent, Jacques Fonesque, back in the 1920s, discovered that a new product, NEON, which obviated the need for a filament, meant that the lighted tubing could be shaped into the form of letters. He was quick to exploit the potential and soon his signs were to be seen all over Paris. The first of these promoted *Cinzano.*

Off his trolley

A Mr Goldman, the owner of a US chain of grocery shops was disappointed to realise that his customers invariably stopped shopping when their baskets got heavy. He enlisted the assistance of a handy man and between them came up with a contraption comprised of wheels attached to a folding chair and a basket where the seat should be.

Demonstrator

Shoppers ignored them until he got someone to wheel them around demonstrating their usefulness. And so, in 1930, the genesis of today's shopping trolley saw the light of day. Now, it too, carries advertising hoarding.

See-through technology

Many of the world's greatest inventions came about by chance. However, some level of expertise was required to bring some of them to successful fruition. Over one hundred years ago a German professor of physics, while working in his laboratory with a cathode-ray tube happened upon a new kind of radiation.

X-ray vision

This he realised could have novel uses. Wilhelm Roentgen christened his discovery "X-rays" and went on to develop them into a means of viewing the interior of the human body.

Negative side effects

This provided a great breakthrough for the medical profession. Unfortunately, it took some 50 years to realise that there was a downside to the innovation and that the procedure, like other forms of radiation, could cause cancer. On the other hand a bonus was that radiation could actually be used to good effect in the treatment of cancer by a technique known as radiotherapy.

Cat got your scan

The above happened during the 1950s while the '60s saw the introduction of the CAT scan (or Computerised Axial Tomography) which, using X-rays, scans the body in slices to produce a three dimensional picture of the various body parts.

Enter NMR

To avoid the negatives associated with radiation, the nuclear age spawned alternative diagnostic methodologies. By using powerful electromagnets it became possible to utilise nuclear magnetic resonance (NMR) imaging and record changes in the body's atoms. The NMR is then subjected to detailed analysis and can enable the production of three-dimensional images

of internal organs.

Caught on radar

Perhaps the most topical issue and one that carries a sting in its tale (sic) is that of the arrival of the radar trap which now has the added peril of penalty points. The inventor of the radar gun was one Sir Robert Watson-Watt.

First on the spot fine

It is a recorded fact that shortly after his invention was introduced he was rushing to fulfil a speaking engagement in which he was going to extol the virtues of radar, and, was caught in the very trap of his own making. He was one of the first motorists to have to pay an on-the-spot fine.

All around you

Just noticing everyday problems, and wanting to resolve them, has been the inspiration for many people in the past to devise inventions.

Sealed in time

In the early 1800s, a purveyor of food in France, Nicolas Appert, tried many ways of getting his foodstuffs to last longer. Almost by accident, he found that, when he sealed food in a jar, *and heated it*, it remained fresh for much longer. In fact, it seemed, it lasted indefinitely.

Heat for health

Half a century later, another French man, the chemist Louis Pasteur while working on another project proved that heating foodstuffs to 57 degrees C killed the harmful micro-organisms that caused the problems.

It just worked!

Nicolas Appert had discovered how to achieve what he wanted 50 years before Pasteur, but did not know why it heating food preserved it.

Frozen in time

In 1900, an American businessman, while travelling in the then wilds of Canada noticed that the people there froze food in winter as a way of storing fresh food.

When defrosted and cooked it tasted pretty good. On his return to the United States he experimented with ways of doing this on a large commercial basis.

Birdseye

Eventually he came up with a satisfactory method. He patented his system that successfully froze fish, meat, fruit and vegetables. His name, Clarence Birdseye. His name lives on, branding a variety of products, as does the method known as pasteurisation, thanks to Louis Pasteur who also gave us penicillin.

Keep your eyes, and mind, open - new opportunities exist for you every day.

Unworn rose

Suntory Ltd, Japan, cracked the DNA code of the rose. In so doing, they have done what no one has been able to do, produce a Blue Rose. Way back in 1840, the horticultural societies in Britain and Belgium offered a prize of half a million francs to the first plant breeder to produce such a rose. It was never won!

Humped

The winner of the top prize at the first international Invention Fair in the Middle East went to a man who produced a robot camel jockey. Now there is no more worry about child jockeys being exploited, the robots are controlled remotely using a laptop and joystick. Race times have improved dramatically.

Some coffee perks

Decaffeinated coffee was first invented in 1903 when a group of researchers successfully came up with a method that extracted the caffeine from the beans without destroying the flavour. The name under which it was marketed, SANKA, is derived from *sans caffeine.*

Orange appeal

These jars had a distinctive orange label and the company supplied cafes with coffeepots with a matching orange collar. Rather unfortunately, for this particular company, this colour then became synonymous with decaffeinated coffee from any supplier. Nowadays the colour could have been registered as a trade mark in its own right thus giving SANKA exclusive rights to its use.

Cheeky choice

One of the biggest selling coffees in the world started out as the brain child of an American salesman. His spare time labours resulted in his developing a method for making instant coffee. He decided that he would call it after the first place to give him a really big order. So he set off pitching it to a large range of establishments.

On the house

The first establishment to order a large quantity was a hotel. The name of that hotel was *Maxwell House*. He thought that better than putting his own name on his creation, his surname was Cheek!

Big earner

Nestle was the first company to invent freeze-dried coffee which it did at the behest of Brazil when that country had a production surplus problem. Today, many millions of people earn their living thanks to the world-wide popularity of this beverage.

On the Telly

The sales of instant coffee really took off in the mid50s with the advent of commercial television. The TV breaks were long enough to make a cup of coffee. The, up-until-then dominant competitor, tea, needed far longer to brew and as a consequence its sales took a terrible hammering.

Bags of tea

This downturn was the catalyst that ultimately spawned the arrival of the tea bag. After oil, coffee is the largest export in the world, Brazil producing 30% plus.

Expressing himself

A native Italian, Mr Gaggia while experimenting with steam under pressure and a spring lever mechanism, devised a new method for making expresso coffee. When his machine was perfected and manufactured en masse he can be said to have been the man behind the arrival of the ubiquitous coffee bar.

Holy inspiring

These, in turn, turned all of us on to acquiring a taste for a variety of offerings from Latte to Frappe. By the way, the now so popular Cappuccino is so called because of the resemblance it holds to the cowl on the habit worn by a Capuchin friar.

How to crack America's best kept secret.

Many years back one of the Tech World's most closely guarded and widely speculated about secrets, by business and media alike, could have been common knowledge if only they had known a little about Intellectual Property structures.

Patent granted

It has reached the marketplace now but not with the projected huge sales volume that was bandied about at the outset. This is what was anticipated back then.

That year (December 18, 2001) a US patent was granted to DEKA Products USA for what was to be branded the SEGWAY.

Leakages

Since the following January, when word started to leak out that a revolutionary new mode of transport, that would not only improve our way of getting about but also the environment, was about to be revealed, weird and fanciful stories abounded.

Battery driven

An amazing American inventor, Dean Kamen, who had already made millions of dollars by inventing drug infusion, insulin delivery and dialysis methodologies, was onto something really big. After a decade of research and development costs of $100 million, Dean was going to give the world a new battery driven vehicle.

Lean back and forward

But this was like no other. Resembling an upright weighing scale where you stand on the platform and read off your weight at stomach height, this contraption substitutes the steering handles for the display portion. Simply step onto it, hold the handles (just like on a bike) then lean forward to go in one direction or lean back to reverse. It's really as simple as that.

Speedy but costly

Moreover you can go up to 27 km per hour for two hours before needing to recharge the battery. It was suggested that it will change the shape of cities, how we commute, reduce pollution levels, global warming, the works!

Suggested use

People will drive to the outskirts of town, take the SEGWAY from the boot of the car (or in the States, the trunk!) and make their way to offices or shops in an environmentally friendly, health, way. Because of the consequent reduction in big automobile traffic, it is speculated that inner city roads can be reduced in size, there can be more pedestrian avenues (which, presumably, will have SEGWAY lanes) and congestion almost eliminated.

Public bodies

Initial interest, and some orders, came from the US Postal Services and other public bodies in the United States who would avail of a more robust, industrial version. The obvious attraction to owners of huge warehouses, aircraft hangers and even ocean going oil tankers that need cheap, nimble forms of transportation means that the target market is immense.

Wait and see

Back then production facilities were being built and output/sales estimates were being deliberated. In keeping with the best entrepreneurial traditions the figures were mind blowing.

However, let's wait and see, the early signs were encouraging.

Endorsements

The likes of Apple's Steve Jobs, Intel's Andy Grove and Amazon's Jeff Bezos tried it and acclaimed it a winner. Some say it will be as big as the PC market and even greater than the Internet. **They were wrong!**

Enquiring minds

Back to the secrecy. Business tycoons and media reporters were doing their damnedest since the first inkling that something huge was in the offing to find out more. Every nook and cranny was searched, every contact and "insider" pressed for a hint of what was to emerge. However the lid was as tight as could be. Then the speculation began.

Wild guesses

The guesses ranged from a spacecraft to a scooter and were mentioned in all types of media, business news to high tech magazines. However, if anyone realised that the information was readily available to read, by anyone who cared to look, then all the secret hype could have been exploded.

Read the patent

Back in October, 1999 you could have walked into the US Patent Office (or accessed its website, www.uspto.gov) and read the entire specification in relation to the invention (US patent No 5,971,091). In the first paragraph of the patent application there is an "Abstract" section which sets out the main attributes of the invention.

Using the head

In addition, on subsequent pages, drawings are shown which will further assist in visualising what the patent is all about. This would have cost them nothing to do and just the use of a little grey matter.

History repeated

But of course we are destined to repeat history. A similar situation existed in the Second World War. The Allies were greatly assisted by the use of the recently invented Radar. Germany was perplexed as to how their rivals could be so efficient in the bombing raids and spotting the Luftwaffe in the dark.

A little knowledge

Had Germany known, it could have sent one of its spies into the British Patent Office and read all they needed to know to mimic, illegally because of patent protection, the Radar system. The outcome of the war could have been so much different. Therefore a little knowledge can be a dangerous thing but conversely a little ignorance can be a protective thing.

Into the future

We now know all about the SEGWAY, there have been photographs and reports in the newspapers. However, a massive move to this new form of transport has not materialised. Why is that? What are the shortcomings?

Get on your bike

If you are inspired with the story and the possibilities that it outlined but did not fulfil, you have an opening to come up with something that will. Put on your thinking cap!

Plain sailing

Remember reading about how Australia won the Americas Cup at sailing? There was tremendous hocus pocus about the keel design of the winning yacht. When it arrived in the US it was figuratively and literally shrouded in secrecy.

Hidden from view

The Aussies put an enormous canvas sheet around the hull to cover the keel design and mounted a round the clock security to ensure no one could take a surreptitious peek. And of course the American media went into a frenzy of speculation, when all they had to do was pay a visit to Uncle Sam's Patent Office.

Chapter 21: Putting It Into Practise

Guest speaker

Let me finish with a story from a scientific gathering at which I was a guest speaker.

Scientific Committee

I was asked by the EU Scientific Committee to deliver a paper on Intellectual Property and marketing to an international workshop on *Personalised Health: The Integration of Innovative Sensing, Textile, Information & Communication Technologies* – (in other words, the synergies between advanced textiles, sensors, nanotechnology and ICT). Attendees included specialists form a wide section of the scientific and medical communities.

Capture imagination

My aim was to present a project that would capture the imagination of all those who attended the gathering.

I decided that the whole project must have high appeal and lend itself to publicity. It would also be a role model that could be emulated internationally

Media potential

This is the sort of initiative that could be further explored and teased out without financial exposure. If it proved to be feasible, it could also advance with limited cost until it was proven to be viable. If such were the case, the publicity machine would be called into play and the profile begins to be disseminated across the media.

With this concept as a template, the same logic could be used in similar ventures, and a series of new businesses could emerge.

Harnessing science to business

Because all of the papers being presented were laying emphasis on science, research and the never-ending plea for greater funding, I wanted to look at the problem from a different perspective. I wanted to inspire the audience with a different approach, one that addressed their needs from a sales and marketing perspective.

A small step for science, a big one for commerce

The excellent work that is being done in medical science advances is to be admired and applauded. In each case the quest is for perfection and to bring the project to its final solution. Along the way milestones may be overlooked, as to their particular merits, because the eyes are focused all the time on the ultimate goal.

Mutuality

The conferences highlighted very many areas of interest and endeavour; some of which parallel, duplicate, overlap and/or complement others.

More funding

A common cry was for more funds to facilitate the continuance of research and development projects. In most instances, funding is hard to come by, slow to arrive and/or limits the rate of progress.

Innovation to the rescue

Strange as it may seem, my contention was that the implementation of intellectual property matters, *from a sales and marketing perspective*, would offer a solution to many areas of concern to my audience.

The importance of branding

It is worth noting that the major marketing success in the world of commerce depends greatly on branding. This is the identity that catches the attention of the consumer and is an intricate part of building loyalty.

Hidden science

In many instances, science lies behind the development of many commercial products. Advertising and promotion sell the benefits and explain how it is to be used but the trade mark is the vital ingredient. Once a purchaser believes in the product or service a buying pattern will be established and recommendations to others follow as a consequence. Marketing companies therefore lay great importance on the brand and the selling message.

Patent potential

In some instances further exclusivity can be obtained by seeking to patent the new offering. There is also Design Registration whereby the design of a product, even its ornamentation, can be protected.

Meeting of minds

These, seemingly disparate matters, may appear at a remove from what the conference was organised to address but, in fact, were mobilised by me to great effect.

Huge commercial opportunities

During the presentations made by the experts it became clear that huge commercial opportunities were evident as asides to the central theme of the project in question.

Recognised by a few

While these may be lost to the bulk of the audience, who were
solely concentrating on the scientific significance of the content, I
was more commercially attuned and saw how this could support
my presentation.

Interplay

Moreover, through the means of cross fertilisation, there was an
opportunity for interplay between some of the advancements and
discoveries being put forward by various presenters. Again, this
synergy was a commercially driven one, rather than one based on
the advancement of science *per se*.

The future is huge

One of the presenters was from British Telecom and laboured
under the luxurious title of a futurologist. He outlined not only the
capabilities that currently exist in his field, (unbeknownst to many
of us), but also looked into the future. The spectacle was not only
alarming but also awe-inspiring. It further provoked the concept of
areas for potential collations with some of the other disciplines
that I envisaged and would use when I spoke.

Collaboration

When I took the stage I reminded the audience of some of the
subject matter from previous speakers. I asked them to consider
taking some ideas a stage further.

An actual product

Replacing the "picture if you will" approach for a more hard-nosed commercial one, a realisable product was created there and then, in front of them. I envisaged them being part of my team that would collaborate in producing an innovative, marketable product. This product was to be branded, packaged and susceptible to all forms of intellectual property protection, perhaps even including patenting. It would be put forward as "ready-for-the-shelf" product.

Built in alarm

The example I used was a nappy designed to detect, when worn, health problems in babies (such as high temperature, skin conditions and maybe even soiling) and would activate a built-in alarm.

Clever weave

A telecom company executive (who was one of the attendees and had spoken of the huge leaps being envisaged) could oversee the inclusion in the weave of the nappy, of whatever is needed to transmit signals to a mobile phone. A variety of electronic and optical sensors can now be woven into fabrics for health monitoring purposes.

Signal sent

When problems are experienced, a signal would be sent to the parent's mobile phone and action could be taken. This might entail the adult going to attend the baby or contacting the baby sitter and issuing appropriate instructions.

Trade mark registrations

If this project was feasible, and the experts said that it was, then we need to create a brand name and do a search to ensure that the trademark was available for registration. Then we needed to apply to register the name. The trade mark I created was NAPPYHAPPY. We coined a slogan, "Put a smile on your baby's"; and we devised a colour combination to go on the packaging. A sound mark – "Ma, Ma" can be registered, just like the others listed above, and a device built into the pack that emits this sound when the pack is lifted up.

Copyright

All of the copy that is created around the product can enjoy copyright protection. The novel get-up and ornamentation of the packaging can avail of design registration exclusivity. It could also be possible to apply for a patent if the necessary requirements were met. Now, the product has a range of protected features that offers great attraction to multinational companies. Not only is it a unique item but potential rivals are faced with an array of statutory hurdles.

Future science

I reinforced my case by sketching out a new scenario.

While the scientific developments to realize this ambition may only be partly achieved to date, it already has licensing potential.

Development funding

This type of collaboration could be a win-win situation for all involved. Blue-chip marketing companies would be prepared to contribute to ongoing research if they were offered first refusal in any new developments that ensue. In this way our research team would be provided with a lump sum plus an ongoing revenue stream from subsequent sales of the product. .

Sales potential

By having an astute commercial awareness overseeing the scientific progress of a variety of ventures, a new dimension can be added to research systems. When augmented with the experience, skill and know-how to add sales appeal to a potential marketable end use a range of opportunities emerge.

So much to gain

The market place has an insatiable appetite for new products and services. To meet that demand, novel avenues will be willingly explored. By using cross-fertilisation of projects coupled with creative and clever presentation of the outcome, enhancing its market appeal; then much is to be gained.

Highlight the benefits

Exciting brands are built on great consumer benefits. Major brand owners are always on the lookout for innovations that will enhance their products' appeal, such as new technologies, that will provide compelling benefits for consumers. Any novel insights into consumer needs are eagerly sought.

Mother appeal

A new functionality, that will create the benefit that can be promised by the brand, and enable the actual delivery of that promise, is what the marketer is after. A great insight message is something that, when heard by the targeted consumer group, is accepted by them as intrinsically right. A classic example of such an insight is the widely acknowledged fact that mothers will go to great lengths to do or buy what's best for their new baby.

Huge sellers

Proctor & Gamble's *Pampers* is the biggest selling diaper in the world. An insight in relation to a *Pampers* consumer is that they will do anything to ensure the safety and comfort of their baby.

Peace of mind

A benefit with the radically innovative *"Pampers"* mentioned above would be – now with, mobile communications, that baby need never be soiled for long. Nor will it be in more serious danger - the *Nappyhappy* will tell when it is time to change or alert them to the more serious problem. Unrivalled peace of mind!

Consumer retention

The brand owner craves consumer loyalty. That comes from having a highly relevant benefit and how well the product delivers against that promised benefit. Great promise, ineffective functionality leaves the consumer disappointed. An ill-conceived benefit, even with great functionality - never gets anyone to try it.

Under-utilised

Some lateral, commercial thinking is called for, which when added to that of their medical/scientific minds, can be a powerful, profitable combination. I said that I hoped that this small introduction to the scope of intellectual property rights, most of which are being under-utilised, will shed some light on the true potential that lies in their hands.

A real catalyst for change

The simple product example should not be taken too definitively but only act as a catalyst for what can emerge if the new, suggested approach is adapted.

It was very well received and became a topic for spirited conversation.

Chapter 22: What You Can Achieve

CONCLUSIONS: HOW ALL THIS HELP YOU ACHIEVE YOUR OBJECTIVES

Positive thoughts

You can now get into the right frame of mind to turn on your creativity. Dismiss all those negative thoughts that you are not good at this type of thing; or you don't have the skills, proper education, technical ability, qualifications and any other barrier you can erect.

Overcome or obviate

If you are alert, you will encounter everyday happenings, problems, snags and difficulties that need to be overcome. You will appreciate how helpful it would be if there was a way to overcome or obviate these annoyances. If so, you will recognise how solutions would be appreciated by others who encounter these problems too.

Use them

In conclusion, do not dismiss out of hand any ideas you may have. Remember, many of the world's great inventions came from people just like you. There is great satisfaction, as well as financial reward, in bringing into being something that you have devised, that is benefit to others.

Healthy income

Keep your hair on: You don't have to be an Einstein to come up with a commercial invention that can provide a very healthy income.

Lateral thinking

Just don't jump to obvious conclusions, have an inventive perspective. For instance, remember this, you can get just as drunk on water as you can on land!

The patent process

You have learned:

> - what will be considered inventive and what will not;
>
> - the three essentials required for a patent,
>
> - how to do a subject matter search,
>
> - how to draft and file your patent application (if you are not going to use a patent attorney)

You have been given links to web sites to use for all of these steps and templates to assist you in completing the required documentation.

Patent pending

The benefits of the patent pending period are familiar to you and the priority advantage that goes with it.

You are also aware of the Patent Cooperation Treaty facility and how it can be used to extend the period before you have to make a final decision on the number of countries in which you wish to file for a patent.

No patent

We explored the potential that is still open to you if you feel that your concept has a limited or no chance of being granted a patent. There is still much that you can use in your protective armoury and marketing strategy.

Testing your skill

You have had the chance to put your brain to the test by devising solutions to challenges set in respect of finding patentable solutions. To augment this exercise you read how these were resolved, and the logic and ingenuity employed.

Trade marks

There are very many ways that trade marks can be brought into play to help your cause. These have been explained and examples of their effectiveness clearly shown. The variety of trade marks and how they offer greater protection to invention was clearly illustrated by numerous examples.

You know how to create, search and file a trade mark. This you can do nationally and internationally (for example, you could opt for the scope of the Community Trade Mark (CTM) that covers 28 member states in one application).

TM and ®

The letters TM can be used by you to great advantage. This differs from the ® designation but you can profit from the misconception generally held regarding the significance of TM.

Branding

The strategy of employing the "Be first and brand it" approach has been set out in great detail. The marketing edge this can arm you with has been explored and detailed to show you how you can mobilise it to your advantage.

National Design rights

Another form of protection can be yours by way of protecting the shape, configuration and ornamentation of a new product. This can give you another defence against possible rivals. It is inexpensive and can be extended for up to 25 years. Your filing can include a number of variations to the design and configuration of the product. There are also unregistered rights.

Registered Community Design

The national design right can be used where you intend to market in one or more particular countries. However, if you intend to file in many countries, you can avail of the RCD. This registration can include all 28 EU member states.

Copyright

This right has been explained in some detail including its scope, duration, and importance to everyone in the creative areas. Although registration is the best and strongest way to protect your trade mark, certain aspects of branding may be protected by copyright, these were discussed.

Ownership

The "who owns what" questions are answered. The rules regarding the ownership of the employer and the employee in copyrighted works have been highlighted as were the penalties for infringement. You were advised to always ensure you have an explicit advance agreement in writing to obviate any confusion that might arise at a later date.

Copyright notice

You were shown how to identify your ownership of your creative work and the provident steps to put others on notice of your rights and your intention to enforce them.

Inspiring stories to assist you

An entire chapter illustrated how inventiveness has come to the surface throughout history - how inventors showed their brilliance, coupled with determination and a spirit to succeed..

Now it's your turn

Armed with all this information and guidance there is every reason for you to begin the exciting adventure to inventiveness. No more excuses. Avoid ever saying

"I should have." Go for it and enjoy.

Connect with Liam M Birkett

My website: liammbirkett.com

Like me on Facebook: facebook.com/liammbirkett

Connect with me on LinkedIn: linkedin.com/in/liambirkett

My Smashwords author profile:
smashwords.com/profile/view/liamBirkett

For a hard copy of this book see http://www.liammbirkett.com/

How to create your trade mark, protect it and build your brand.

The book that saves you time and money.

LIAM M BIRKETT

Learn how to go about devising your trade mark. The essential steps to ensure that you can use, register and protect it. Read how easy it is to add value to your brand and use branding to get free publicity.

Quick Guide

TO BUILDING
AND PROTECTING
YOUR BRAND

The ebook that saves you time and money.

LIAM M BIRKETT

Learn how to go about devising your trade
mark. The essential steps to ensure that you
can use, register and protect it.

Quick Guide

To Becoming An

Inventor

This ebook will inspire you to be an active inventor.
Unlock your ideas and turn them into profitable reality.
It shows you how to go through the stages from concept to sales.
It tells you how to limit the downside risk and offers you a
variety of options to your same objective – success.

Liam M Birkett

Made in the USA
Lexington, KY
27 April 2016